Reader Comments

"I am a high school math teacher. I was given a new course to teach last year for the first time. I decided to teach the students about personal finance. As I was doing research for the course, I came across your newsletter and have been using it ever since as part of my class. The students are really glad that I have made this a part of the class and keep asking for more."

—Beth Beto

"A day without reading DebtSmart® is like a day without sunshine. Thanks again for the wonderful job you do and all the valuable information you pass on to the public...I have learned so much from your articles, keep them coming."

—Diane Ayers, NC

"The articles were well written; in plain English, with facts and information that did not overwhelm an individual. Keep up the good work. Thanks!!"

—Linda Davis, AZ

"I love your newsletter. My husband and I put a hold on our credit reports so the banks don't get our information anymore and we don't get the 500 a day offers."

—Leslie

"You rock! My resolution for 2002 is to-pay-down-the-damn-Visa-balance-even-though-I-have-a-9.9%-fixed-rate-Platinum-Capital- One-card!!!"

—Kim

"I love the newsletter. It is very informative about debt reduction, as well as, realistic about debt and the fact that people have it."

—Darryl

"I have gained so much knowledge from the newsletter. It is hard to put into words, the thanks and appreciation I feel, taking the time to educate the public about debt. Keep up the good work and one day the subscribers will be debt free."
—Diane

"I am continually grateful that you have such drive and dedication and creativity. You and your staff are providing a wonderful service to the American people."

—Barbara

"I enjoy this newsletter a lot, it helps me feel like I am at least trying to become as informed as possible...when I do make a major purchase I know all I should about interest rates and my credit report, payments, etc....and PROUD to say I have not used a major credit card in a year! Thanks from this ever-learning single woman."

—Linda

"Great newsletter for me personally and for low income families that I work with to help them to become self sufficient!"

—Susie

"Most of the websites who are allegedly there to help us with being debt-smart are ACTUALLY just trying to sell you something (such as yet ANOTHER credit card!). I have learned so much here at DebtSmart®. You guys are the best!"

—Pam

"Great Newsletter! The info is always timely and relevant to my credit situation, and I look forward to each issue. As to number of credit cards, in my count I've learned we have a total of 10, but most have not even been activated. Lately I've been an "intro-hopper", taking advantage of much-lower APRs, to get rid of CC debt (in 9/98 owed 29k, now owe 6.1k, so it won't be much longer). Snowballing, lowering APRs, transferring as credit score improves, all are working, and your advice always helps. Thanks!"

—Dan E.

"I love the newsletter. I am in debt and am trying to get out. I find lots of tidbits of information that I can use and pass on. My friends also agree."

—Danielle

"I was divorced 4 years ago. I had a husband who took care of all the bills for the most part, and now I am taking control of what little amount I do have to myself. There is a feeling of great accomplishment and pride that goes with my being able to take care of myself 4 years later and have made some wise decisions with your help. Thank you so much! Your online help is available when "I" have time to read up on the information, when I am fully able to sit down and comprehend what choices I have. I have gotten an equity loan to transfer my balances of my charge accounts so that the interest on the loan will be tax deductible, and also to have a new roof put on my home instead of just borrowing the money and the amounts of my finance charges going to pure waste. I never knew any of this 4 years ago let me tell ya...I have been able to increase my monthly cash flow so I feel more secure, and able to pay off the loan faster or take care of unexpected things that happen. You have given this blonde some great advice and I do appreciate your help... thank you, thank you, thank you!"

How to be more

CREDIT CARD AND DEBT SMART

Powerful financial management strategies for saving money on your credit cards and debt!

Volume 1

Scott Bilker

PRESS ONE PUBLISHING Barnegat, New Jersey

How to be more
CREDIT CARD AND DEBT SMART

Powerful financial management strategies for saving money on your credit cards and debt!

Volume 1

by Scott Bilker

Published by:

PRESS ONE PUBLISHING
PO Box 563, Barnegat, NJ 08005-0563
Tel: (609) 660-0682 **Fax:** (609) 660-1412
E-mail: scott@DebtSmart.com
URL: http://www.DebtSmart.com

Copyright © 2002 by Scott Bilker
First Printing 2002, PDF Electronic Version 2002
10 9 8 7 6 5 4 3
Printed in the United States of America

Publisher's Cataloging-in-Publication
   (Provided by Quality Books, Inc.)

Bilker, Scott.
   How to be more credit card and debt smart. Volume 1 :
  powerful financial management strategies for saving
  money on your credit cards and debt! / Scott Bilker.
     p. cm.
   Includes index.
   LCCN 2002107198
   ISBN 0-9648401-3-8

   1. Credit cards--United States. 2. Consumer credit--
United States. 3. Finance, Personal--United States.
I. Title.

HG3756.U54B546 2002   332.024'02
                  QBI02-200476

For all the readers of DebtSmart ®

Table of Contents

Warning—Disclaimer

CHAPTER 1

CREDIT CARDS

"Credit cards don't kill people, people kill people."—Scott Bilker, 2001

Lower Your Credit-Card APR Right Now!

When was the last time you took a look at your credit card APR (Annual Percentage Rate)? You may think you know what the bank is charging you for the use of their money, but you might be surprised to find that terms have changed and you're now paying as much as 18 to 20%. The U.S. average is around 18%, and I believe that is much more than you have to pay—especially when you've been a good customer with that bank.

So what do you do if you discover that you are paying too much for your loans? Well, quite simply, make the bank lower your rate. Sound impossible? More than half of the time I've been able to make my banks lower their interest rates. The trick is to have the right deal-breaker.

A deal-breaker or BATNA (best alternative to a negotiated agreement), as William Ury, author of "Getting Past No," would say, is what you will do if you don't get your way. It's the threat of leaving the car dealership if they don't agree to your price, or the I'll-call-my-lawyer option if you can't settle a dispute.

Some of you might be thinking, "What kind of threat can I deliver to my credit-card bank to make them lower my rate? What deal-breaker do I have?" Realize that there are options, and start taking advantage of them. The first place to look is in your mailbox.

You know those low-rate transfer credit-card offers that go from your mailbox straight to the "circular file"? Banks attempting to get you to switch sent out more than 3 billion transfer offers last year, so I know you've seen them. Take a closer look at the next one that arrives—probably today. The best part about that offer is that you need not apply for the new credit line in order to make good use of it.

What that offer becomes to you is the deal-breaker—the leverage you might need to persuade your current bank to lower its APR on your account. How?

Take out your credit card, flip it over, and call the customer-service number on the back. After you're done going through the torture of entering your credit card-number and information in the automated voice menu, choose the option that gets you to a human. Remember to be calm yet firm. Your conversation could go something like this:

Account rep: "How can I help you today?"

You: "I've been looking closely at my credit-card statement, and I've noticed that your bank has been charging me like 18% interest for a while now. I don't believe I should be paying that much interest."

Account rep: "What would you like me to do?"

You: "Lower my APR to something more reasonable, like 6.9%."

That might be all it takes to make them lower your rate, but I want to prepare you for a bigger battle.

Account rep: "I can't do that?"

You: "Who can?"

Account rep: "Nobody really, we can't just change rates like that."

You: "Can I speak to your supervisor, please?"

Account rep: "Sure, please hold."

Supervisor: "Can I help you?"

You: "Your bank is charging me way too much interest, and I want it lowered to something like 6.9%. This is the deal: I'm holding a credit offer in my hand from [*name the bank*] bank. And they're willing to give me 4.9% for 6 months, no annual fee [*read the offer terms*]. I bet your bank has better offers for new, unproven customers than they do for established profitable ones, don't they? I see no reason to stay with [*name*] bank if they're not willing to treat me better. I have plenty of other banks to choose from."

Supervisor: "You know that if you take that offer, the rate will go up in six months."

You: "Well, I'll worry about that six months from now. And that's six months without any high interest charges from your bank. Or six months that your bank doesn't make any money from my account."

Supervisor: "What can I do for you?"

You: "Look, I'm not asking for you to lower my rate to 4.9%, but I do need a reason to keep my balance with your bank. How about 6.9% or 7.9%?"

Now, at this point your chances are 50/50 as to whether they are going to lower your rate. Your bank may come back with an offer like 7.9% for six months or a low-annual-fee card at a lower rate. In general, you should always take the lower rate, even if there's a time limit. You can always call back in six months and do this again.

Remember that you need a real credit offer to do this. Without a deal-breaker you're just begging, and you won't win by begging. Success here may also depend on how good you've been at handling your account—paying on time. But no matter what your credit history is, you should make that call, because you may be surprised to find that the bank really wants to keep you as a customer.

It cost banks plenty of money to find a new customer. The competition for a piece of your credit business is intense. Banks are fighting to get you to switch, so it is truly in their best interest to keep you, a proven and profitable customer.

How much can you save? Here's some incentive to make that call today. Let's say your current rate is 18%. If you can get your bank to drop its rate to something even as high as 9.9%, you'll save a bundle! The dollar amount saved depends on two other factors: (1) how much you owe and (2) how much you're paying per month.

For example, if you owe $5,000 and you're making payments of $100, at 18% it's going to take 93 months to pay off the card, and it's going to cost $9,300. However, at the new rate of 9.9% it takes only 65 months to pay off the card, for a total cost of $6,500. You save the difference between $9,300 and $6,500, which is $2,800!

That's $2,800 for making a phone call—do it now!

Payment Order Counts When Saving Money On Your Debt

A big myth in credit card and loan repayment is to "start with the smallest debt" and work your way to the largest.

I have been asked repeatedly about this debt-repayment strategy during radio interviews and directly, and the only reason I can think of that some people may pay the smallest debts first is for purely psychological reasons. They want to feel like they're wiping out their debt, and it may seem faster to start with the smallest debt, but the reality is that it may take longer.

The advice that one should "start with the smallest debt" when applying payments should never be used as a rule of thumb. Paying the smallest debt first is only good when the smallest debt happens to be the debt with the highest interest rate. If that's not the case, then paying the smallest debt first can be a costly mistake.

The least expensive way to apply payments to your debt is to pay the most toward the highest-interest-rate loans (that's the rule). Here's an example that illustrates exactly what's going on:

Say you have two debts: $11,000 at 18% APR with a minimum monthly payment of $220, and another loan of $7,000 at 6.9% APR with a minimum payment of $140. You also have a total of $500 per month available to pay toward both loans, and you want to apply the payments in the most efficient way to each debt.

Strategy 1: Pay the smallest debt first.

The most you can allocate to pay toward the "smallest debt" is $280, because you must make minimum payments of $220 on the larger debt ($280+$220=$500). If you make the payments in those amounts, the "smallest debt" ($7,000) is paid off in 27.07 months. During this time you are paying $220 toward the $11,000 debt, which will now have a balance of $9,180.

Q&A: Negotiating a Payoff

Question

Scott,
I was told that I could call my older credit card banks, and "negotiate" a payoff of the account if I close the account. Is this true, and if so how will it impact my credit rating?
—Ken

Answer

Ken,

You can always negotiate anything! Pick up the phone and call today!

Negotiating won't impact your credit rating. If you're concerned about that then ask the bank what they are going to report. In the incredibly remote possibility that they say they'd report something negative just make it part of the negotiated deal then they don't report anything. Be sure to keep good notes about whom you spoke with and what they agreed to do. Something in writing is always best.
—Scott

Q&A: Transfer Credit Card Balances

Question

My husband and I filed for bankruptcy in 1995. Since then we have established good payment records with high interest credit card companies. I'm ready to drop them and transfer my balances to a lower interest rate card(s). When I start looking on the net, I see introductory rates for first time applicants with good credit. I'm having a hard time finding cards with the transfer option.

I've had my existing accounts for several years (or more), plus we just bought a house, so I think we deserve better interest rates. I called my accounts personally, but they don't offer better rates, only a larger line of credit. I have enough credit already.
—Penny

Answer

Penny,

First of all Penny I'd like to say that I agree that you do deserve a better rate!

As you may know, bankruptcy stays on your credit report for 10 years. That means that all the banks know that you've had problems in the past, but that's long ago at this point, and I am sure there are banks that may be willing to give you a better deal.

The important issue now is how you've been handling your credit for the past few years. From what you've said my feeling is that you've been doing a good job with paying on time. That being my assumption it's time for the banks to give you a better deal or you should take your business elsewhere!

So you've already called your current banks and they won't budge on the rates. Try this, call them back and explain it this way, "I've just received a transfer offer in the mail for 1.9% and I'm going to take it if you don't reduce my rate. I've been happy dealing with your bank but it's just getting too costly. I'd be willing to stay a customer, but I need some type of reduction in my rate or I'll just have to take my business to another bank."

If the first rep you get on the phone cannot help you then ask to speak to a supervisor. If the supervisor says that they cannot lower the rate, then find out why and make it clear that they lost your business. WE MUST PUNISH THEM!!

Now, you mentioned that you have a few accounts. If the first bank won't lower the rate then call another account and transfer the balance from the first bank to this account. Tell the second bank, "If you give me a good deal on a balance transfer, right now, I'll do it." Well, at this point you should do it anyway. Just be sure to punish the first bank for not lowering the rate. Then, after the first bank doesn't have your business for a while you can give them a call and let them know that you're ready to start using them again if they give you a better rate or a transfer offer.

As far as the online offers go, it can sometimes be very difficult to get those low rate deals when applying online. I suggest you try in your snail-mailbox. That's where I always get the best offers. Actually, the best offers are from my current banks but there are other good offers from new banks all time. Last year banks mailed 3 billion offers to us consumers!

Never forget that no matter what your situation YOU are the customer and they should be treating you with the philosophy of "the customer is always right." There's a lot of competition out there for our business so let's all make them work to keep us satisfied!

—Scott

Q&A: Annual Fees

Question

Scott,
Is it true that when you get a credit card offer that has an annual fee, it's not a good credit card? I have gotten some in the mail from Capital One and I would really like to get the 0% but I don't want to pay the annual fee. Are there credit cards out there with 0% intro that don't require an annual fee? if so can you name a few. Thanks, I enjoyed you show on CN8!
—Patricia

Answer

Patricia,
Thanks for watching the show on CN8—glad you enjoyed it!

All that matters, the way I see it, is that the card can save you money. Just because there is an annual fee doesn't mean the card is bad. If the annual fee is $500 then I would say it's bad. You really have to do the math for your situation.

Say you had a 0% APR card with a rate that never changes. Sounds good doesn't it?

Say it has an annual fee of $29...not to bad. But say the credit limit is $200. Then the annual fee becomes expensive because even if you max out the card at 0% the $29 annual fee makes the APR go from 0% to 14.5%!

I really focus on the math and how to know the true cost of credit offers in my book, *Credit Card and Debt Management*. It's so important to be able to uncover all these costs so you can compare credit offers.

Now say you had a $10,000 limit on a 0% APR for one year with a $100 annual fee. It sounds like an expensive annual fee but if you use the entire limit the TRUE APR for the first year is only 1%.

—Scott

Q&A: Drowning in debt

Question

Dear Scott,
I am drowning in debt. I am attempting to figure out a budget that is livable. WE have a daughter going to college next fall, a grown son that has moved back home and a son who has moved out but we cosigned for his truck payment so we are stuck with that. I was tempted to order your book but I have gotten so many debt books but nothing that will help me. I looked at our credit card debt which is more than I make in a year. I work but had a second job that is not working out. My husband works full-time. We just need help in figuring out what to do. Thanks for at least listening.
—Jeanie

Answer

Jeanie,
Thanks for writing!

Sounds like you really have your hands full...each of the situations you're dealing with requires much work to resolve. I hope that I can provide you with some useful ideas.

Daughter in college

I don't have to mention how expensive college is becoming. It's already double the cost then when I attended just 10 years ago. Make sure you look into financing options right away. You can find out about the details of government backed loans at the Department of Education web site at http://www.ed.gov/.

Also, consider having your daughter attend a community college for the first two years. Most of the credits would probably transfer to four-year colleges. I took this route and it saved me thousands of dollars in tuition!

Son who moved back home

I have been buried by debt before so I know how tough it is to deal with. If I had a grown son who moved back home at that time I would ask him to contribute to the family, financially. I wouldn't want to ask but sometimes you have no choice.

Truck payments

From the way you mentioned this it sounds like there is no chance that you're going to be able to get any money at all for the truck payments. Can you convince him to sell the truck and get a less expensive vehicle?

Debt in general

Getting debt under control is about getting organized, creating a plan, being disciplined and following your plan, limiting spending, and taking advantage of your best loan options to reduce the cost of the debt by lowering your interest rates. I think that you're doing the right thing by learning about credit and taking action to pay back debt.

Sometimes, even after a good plan, you may not be able to get the debt under control, then it may be time to consider other options, maybe even bankruptcy. You can learn more about bankruptcy from Nolo.com.

Another option is credit counseling. Just be sure to read all the details in their agreements before signing up. If you have any questions about a particular company just let me know. Try looking at American Consumer Credit Counseling (ACCC).

Good luck and please keep in touch to let me know what happens!

—Scott

Q&A: Extending a Low Rate

Question

Scott,

In the past year I left a considerably higher paying job for which I was in six years, to take a less stressful and lower paying one. Consideration of debt was a difficult one in this transition. I knew I would now be making less money to pay off the debts incurred but never realized how difficult it would be. I am now paying the minimum required and know that I will never get out of it this way. Any suggestions? Have moved most debt to lower rate cards, but the time on those is running out. Can I request that my rate remain the same since I make my payments on time?

—Nancy

Answer

Nancy,

You can request that your rates be lowered but they're not going to do it unless you give them a good reason. That reason is that you'll transfer your balance to another bank unless they lower your rate.

Now that you have a lower-stress job you may want to consider earning extra money in your spare time. I know many people that have successfully cleaned up they're house plus made some extra cash selling their old stuff on eBay.com.

Also, be sure to make a complete list of all your financial obligations, mortgage/rent, phone, credit cards, cable TV, etc. and figure out how that works with your current income. This list of monthly payments is part of the roadmap you'll need to make the right financial decisions.

—Scott

Q&A: Fighting an Increasing Rate

Question

Scott,

I had a card that had a fixed rate of 5% on my balance. I closed the account years ago when I started taking control of my debt. Since this was the lowest rate of the cards I had I was only paying the minimum and concentrating instead on paying off other high interest credit. I received a notice with one of my invoices that they would be increasing the rate to 20% and that I basically didn't have a choice in the matter (fine print). I transferred the balance over to other cards that would have a lower APR than the 20% they would be imposing however this severely limited my available credit for emergency purposes.

Just wanted to know if it is legal for them to increase the rate on a closed account and if there was any other option for me to consider. Obviously this would be information for any future similar situations. Thanks!

—Mike

Answer

Mike,

Do you have the original paperwork that gave you the fixed rate of 5%? I truly hope so because it's that documentation that could ultimately help you keep that rate. The only problem is that you did transfer the balance but you did so because you thought they wouldn't keep the rate at what they promised.

I see this happen frequently, that's why I ALWAYS keep copies of the letter, terms, conditions, etc. in my files for just such a situation. I even photocopy applications!

If this happened to me, and I found evidence that they couldn't raise the rate, then I might even contact a lawyer and see what could be done. I would also contact the Federal Trade Commission and other consumer groups to see if they could help me make the bank honor their agreement.

For the future...get everything in writing and keep it in a file!

Good luck and please let me know what happens.

—Scott

Q&A: Make Them Compete

Question

Dear Scott,
How do you lower the interest rate charged to something more reasonable??? Along with this, how do you lower the monthly payment to something more manageable??
—Larry

Answer

Larry,

The best way to lower your rates is to make banks compete for your business! Call your current banks and let them know that if they don't give you reasonable rates you'll take your business somewhere else!

Keep low interest rate offers that you get in the mail so you have more options and bargaining power.

You can lower your payments by paying the minimum but that will increase the long-term cost of each debt. However, that's okay if and when you have no choice. I would question someone making minimum payments so they can go on vacation to Hawaii. :)

—Scott

CHAPTER 2

GETTING ORGANIZED

"Organization is the key to success with anything."—Scott Bilker, 2000

9 Steps to Get Organized for Financial Success!

The beginning of my financial life was when I received my driver's license. Before that I rode my bicycle around and had no bills. Well, I needed a car, right? I had to get to work so I could pay for the car, to get to work. That's what started the bill cycle. The car was used (preowned) but it was the gas credit card that was getting charged.

Let's not forget that I could now go to the mall, buy stuff, and take Larissa on better dates than McDonalds (we started dating before I could drive). So it didn't take long for the bills to start arriving in the mail.

I just didn't know what to do with this mail. Nobody ever showed me a system for managing bills because I didn't have any to keep organized.

So what did I do back then? Probably what many people do today. Bring in the mail, stack it on a desk, and tend to the pile at the last minute. Hopefully I didn't miss too much because I frequently found mail on the floor behind the desk.

It didn't take long for me to realize that I had to do something. I had to get organized!

That was a lifetime ago, really, I was 18 then, now I'm 35 and insanely organized about handling money, bills, and all finances. I've learned over the years that the better organized you are with all your transactions the less likely you are to:

- Bounce checks.
- Exceed credit limits.
- Pay late.
- Get charged for stuff you didn't buy.
- Get hooked into extra charges.
- Be stressed over bills.

- Go into perpetual debt.
- Let fraud go unnoticed.

Here are the 9 quick steps to getting organized for financial success—today!

1) Filing system.

When it comes to getting organized, everything needs a place, a home, a spot. The basic filing cabinet is the best way to organize the paperwork.

The hanging files are the best. They're just easier to work with, easier to access. A basic filing cabinet costs around $30 and is well worth the price.

Once you have a filing cabinet, and some hanging files, create a file for each bill and bank account, for example, mortgage/rent, electric, cable TV, water/sewer, health clubs, checking account, savings account, cash receipts, etc. For credit cards I name the file by the bank name and the last four digits of the card number, i.e., "Citibank 4323."

Lastly, create one more file called, "Bills Unpaid." This is the place to put all those annoying statements until you have time to write the checks.

2) Take care of the mail when it arrives.

Don't let the mail pile up! As soon as you bring in the daily stack of bills, which is what most of it is anyway, go through each envelope immediately. What I do is open every bill, throw away all the stuff that's not important, and staple the bill to the bill-payment envelope, then put then in the bills in the Bills Unpaid file

Now when you're ready to sit down and take care of payment, all your bills will be in place and you won't have to spend time going through each envelope before writing the check.

3) Use accounting software.

I know everyone reading this article right now has a computer. That means you should be using software to track your spending and organize your financial life. I cannot think of a better use of the computer for people in general!

"If you have a computer, then you should be using financial software." That's a quote.

Why?

Money is like the blood of your financial life. It flows into every aspect of what you do. It circulates in, out, and all around everyone in the family. By using your computer to track spending, you'll always know exactly what's going on, where money is being spent, and how to plan for new purchases.

The most powerful aspect about using software is eliminating that checking ledger. I haven't written in a check ledger since 1987! I have searchable records of every credit card charge and check that I've written in my entire life!

The best part is that I don't bounce checks. It's easy to balance your checking account using the computer. There's no adding, subtracting, etc. You just match the checks (and ATM withdrawals) with your bank statement and everything should balance. If it doesn't then you can quickly find the problem.

You know how you sometimes get a bill that you think you've already paid? It's very easy to find out by doing a search with the computer.

A word of caution: if you do use software then you MUST back up that data! It won't take long for you to completely abandon those paper ledgers, but PLEASE make a back up EVERY time you work on your bills!

Keep in mind that tracking alone won't solve money problems. For example, in 1995 I created a report for the year that detailed all my spending by category. I spent 18% of my income on the mortgage, 11% on groceries, 9% for utilities, 6% on federal tax, 6% on social security tax, 6% on property tax, 5% on medical.

Those are the top-spending categories which, used more than 50% of my income for the year. I cannot make changes in any of those categories unless I decided to sell my house, or cut back on food. Tracking lets me know where the money is going, but I have limited control over those categories. Areas I can change don't really add up to much, like 1.4% for entertainment.

4) Enter the transactions into the computer.

The software will not be helpful unless you enter the transactions. A strategy for accomplishing this is to put all credit card receipts in the Bills Unpaid file as soon as you get home from shopping. Then you can enter these transactions into the computer on the same day you pay bills.

Entering your transactions in the computer is the confirmation that your perception of what's going on matches your bank's. That means that your computer shows should be what's correct, and the credit card statement better match what your computer says or there's a mistake somewhere. It's your way to make sure you really did charge every item and write every check. It's the way to detect fraud and bank mistakes!

5) Pay bills on a specific day.

The one lesson I learned early on is that I didn't want to be tortured by dealing with bills every single day. That's why I put the bills in the Bills Unpaid file, and that's why I choose to pay bills once every two weeks—on pay day, always a good time, when I had the money. :)

It usually takes me about 2 to 3 hours to pay my personal bills once every two weeks. Once I start on this task I'm focused! I review every single credit card statement, check, transaction, credit offer, etc. to make sure that I'm receiving the best rates and lowest cost credit options.

Each transaction is carefully recorded in the computer. It's important that on this "bill pay day" everything matches. My billing statement matches what I have in the computer and all accounts balance. All check numbers line up so there are no missing checks.

6) Balance your checking account.

I've already mentioned this point, however I cannot stress it enough. Many people do not balance accounts and it's very costly if you don't. The consequences: bouncing checks. The fees for this can be as high as $35 from your bank and $35 from the bank of the person who you wrote the check to.

By balancing your accounts and using software to handle transactions you can easily avoid an incident that happened to a friend of mine. She accidentally wrote two checks for her mortgage and the mortgage company cashed both. The result was that ALL her other checks bounced like super balls! The cost, when the smoke cleared, for those bounced checks was more than $800 plus the aggravation of dealing with all the banks, freezing of accounts, and stress.

7) Create a list of all bills and debts.

One sheet of paper listing all bills, debts, due dates, contact phone, etc. is one of most powerful tools for financial success! I've included many of these worksheets in my best-selling book, *Credit Card and Debt Management*.

Each time you pay bills be sure to update the list. I started out with a list on paper then I moved to using Excel. Now, because I have so many credit cards, I had to create an Access database to track that information.

You need this list to be your roadmap. It's a planning tool for future spending. You'll be able to see your spending plans at a glance.

8) Create a list of credit offers.

You know that "junk mail" from your credit cards? Well some of those low rate offers are actually VERY good! I always keep a list of current offers from my all of my active credit card accounts. Usually, half of my credit cards are offering me transfer deals less than 5.99%! Some are even a true 0%!

I also keep a list of new credit card offers; however, I do prefer to take advantage of the offers from my current banks since I have a long history of doing business with them, giving me more bargaining power.

The key here is to create these lists. This way, if one of your current credit cards raises their rate, you don't have to look very far to find a better deal. You don't have to keep a stack of mail to go through. You simply pull out the list and start calling!

9) Start a financial notebook.

I keep all my notes on the computer but there was a time when I actually wrote in a book, how barbaric is that! :)

Whether by hand or in a computer this is very important! You need to have detailed notes when you contact your credit card banks, checking bank, mortgage company, etc.

The reason is that sometimes the phone reps don't make the proper notes in your account, and you'll need to reference your notes to keep all those banks in line.

Your financial notebook should include your strategies, for example, "Be sure to transfer the $2,000 balance from the Discover card to the Advanta 3.9% offer by 11/25." The beauty of keeping an organized notebook is that you can refer to your notes, which means you don't have to think about all the details all the time.

So there you have it. I have followed these steps for financial organization for years with incredible results. I've keep my interest costs down, I only have to deal with bills and payment one day every two weeks, I rarely bounce checks, I have corrected many bank errors (never in my favor of course), and I don't have to think about financial details on a moment-to-moment basis.

7 Steps for Eliminating Your Debt

Many people may say that shedding debt is common sense: "Pay for everything in cash and don't incur any debt." Yeah, sure, easily said when you have a household income of 70 to 80 thousand (and no kids). Obviously the best way to handle your finances is to pay for everything with cash. Not everyone has that luxury.

I don't know anyone who purchased their home with cash. There are also other situations that arise-like medical and family emergencies, unexpected car failure, and the list goes on. Just because you have some debt, doesn't necessarily imply that you've mismanaged your entire financial life.

Once you suspect that your debt is starting to get as large as the federal government's, you may want to consider a quick diet for debt reduction.

Step 1: Stop incurring more debt-unless it's an emergency.

One thing I really hate doing is telling people how to spend their money. I prefer to help people identify the best lending deals. Unfortunately, the truth is that if you want to freeze your debt, you must freeze your spending, especially if you don't have the income to support that debt. No spending, no debt. Real simple.

Step 2: Evaluate your financial condition-get a plan.

"If you fail to plan, you plan to fail," that's a guarantee. Creating a plan involves many steps, like taking a close look at each and every creditor you owe, understanding exactly how much it's costing you to have each particular debt, and reviewing your payment history with all creditors (did you pay on time).

Your plan must be a roadmap that takes you from debt to debtless. To do that you need to know how much your total debt is and how long it will take to pay it off, given your current payments. Once you know that, you can look forward to the day when your debt is gone!

Step 3: Realize there are money-saving options available and keep your eye out for those opportunities.

Ever notice that when you become interested in buying a particular car you suddenly see cars of that model driving around, where before you didn't see any? Well, those cars didn't just get there; they've been there all along. The same is also true when you start searching for debt-reduction options. As you start to dig into debt management and closely examine your situation, you'll start seeing many opportunities to save money. For instance, those low-rate, credit card offers that you find in your mailbox almost every day.

Last year alone, banks mailed some 2.5 billion of these offers. Many of them will save you money, but you need to read the fine print and be able to calculate if their offer is truly something you can use to your advantage.

Step 4: TAKE ACTION!

Knowledge is useless unless you put your plan into action. Don't be lazy! Formulate your money-saving plan today and, most importantly, follow through on it! Simply knowing the route from your home to your destination won't get you there until you actually start traveling.

Step 5: Track credit card offers and loan offers.

You know those low rate offers I was talking about before? Well, you need to track them and save them in a box or file. When you need to turn to another bank for cheaper financing, you'll have already done the research and know which banks to contact. Many who have already pre-approved your application. Also, you need to track offers from your existing credit accounts. They'll be the easiest to take advantage of since you already have a history with them-hopefully a clean, on-time payment history.

Step 6: Don't be hasty in closing credit-card accounts.

When you cut up your credit cards, you cut out your options. As long as your current credit-card accounts (and lines of credit) aren't charging you any fees for inactivity, then it's in your best interest to hang on to that account. What I do is put zero-balance cards in a file called the "credit-card graveyard." When an offer comes along that saves me money, I "exhume" them.

The problem with closing your accounts is that you will be at the mercy of whatever bank(s) you decide to keep. That's the same as saying that you'll shop at one store no matter how good the prices are at other stores. Don't give any bank a monopoly on your business; keep you options open.

Step 7: PAY ON TIME-no matter what it takes!

If there is sin in debt repayment, it is paying late. This hurts you immediately with late fees, which would have been better used to reduce your debt, and a strike against your future bargaining power. But most importantly, if you pay late you may not be able to get the best rates and deals when you need them most; like on a mortgage. In the long run, that kind of negligence can cost you thousands of dollars. I would, and have, borrowed money to make sure my payments get there on time. The result is that my rates have been under 8% APR for all my credit cards for the last 10+ years.

Debt management is a continuous process so stay on top your situation and keep more of your money!

Credit Surfing Saves You Money

What is credit surfing? It's the continuous process of jumping from one low-rate credit card to another every time you have a chance. Does it make sense to do this? Probably, if you carry balances on one or more cards, you need to keep your rates as low as possible because that APR is the key factor in what you're paying in finance charges.

How much do you really save by transferring balances from one card to another? Is "credit surfing" worth the trouble? Let's take a look at how much you would save by transferring $3,000 from a 19.8% credit card to 5.9% for only 6 months.

Before we begin to find the savings, it is necessary to identify more information. Specifically, we must know all loan variables and fees in order to make an exact comparison. Also, we must keep the payment amounts consistent when comparing loans. Let's say you're paying the minimum payment of 2% of today's balance for the entire 6 months and there are no transfer fees, which is common, and no annual fee. In this case the monthly payments are $60.

Remember that all money is the same no matter who lends it to you. It's just green paper that you can use to buy stuff with. Therefore, the only difference between lenders is really the cost of the loan. I want to define the best loan as being the cheapest—the loan that costs the least, the loan with the lowest amount of overall fees. The way to determine the true savings is to find the amount still owed in both cases after the 6-month trial offer.

If you leave the balance on the 19.8% card and make 6 monthly payments of $60, the amount owed after the 6th payment is $2,934.

Another way to view this is that you paid off only $66 of the original principal ($3,000) in 6 payments of $60. You can view that as only one payment going toward paying the principal, and the other 5 payments being the fee, or the bank's profit in interest charges. After all, it cost you $360 (6x$60) to pay off $66 of that loan. This means that only 18% of the payments went toward the loan and the other 82% of payments were fees. How can you ever expect to pay off a loan when you're paying 82% in fees?

Now let's see what happens if we take advantage of the 5.9% offer for the 6-month trial period. If you transfer the $3,000 balance to the 5.9% card for 6 months and continue to pay $60 per month, your balance after 6 payments is $2,725!

In this case you paid off $275 of the loan which means that 76% of the $360 in payments went toward the loan's principal, while only 24% went to fees, obviously a dramatic improvement. Also, you can view this as almost five of the six payments going toward lowering the principal amount and only a little more than one payment being the fee.

By transferring the balance and taking advantage of this offer, the savings total $209! And even if the bank raised the rate after the 6-month period, you still keep the $209 in savings, which is realized as a decrease in the loan amount. This is a good move even if there was a $50 fee to get that rate.

In my example, this process takes about half an hour to complete, and when it's over you save $209. It's like getting paid $418 an hour to do the transaction! You tell me if it's worth the trouble.

Q&A: Paying Off a Loan with Credit Cards

Question

Scott,
I have a home eq. loan for 10 years at 8.50% for $26,000.00. Could I pay this down with credit cards using $500.00 a month payments?
—J.G.

Answer

J.G.,
       I think a better strategy is going to be to get another loan to pay this off. After all, 8.5% ARR is a fairly good rate so you may have some trouble beating this rate with credit cards over a ten year period. It can be done as long as you have enough credit to continually get good, true, low rate offers.
—Scott

Q&A: Payment Order

Question

Scott,
I have 3 credit cards with a total debt of $25000. I am paying $950 a month (double the minimum amt due). Should I repay the highest interest card off first, or should I repay the lowest interest card off first and transfer the balance from the higher interest card?
—Nadiyah

Answer

Nadiyah,
       Always, always, always, pay the highest interest rate first. Paying in any other order will definitely cost more money.
       I have heard many "experts" suggest to pay the shortest term loans first or the lowest balance cards first but they're wrong, absolutely wrong!
       Pay the highest rates first.
       I guess you can tell that I really want to get that point across.
       Also, if you can you should transfer from the high rate card to the low rate card. Be careful to make sure, by calling the bank first, that you will get the low rate when you do the transfer. Sometimes the transfer rate may be greater than your current low rate.
       By the way, great question!
       Talk to you later.
       Great to hear that you're able to pay off the debt—keep up the good work!
—Scott

CHAPTER 3

PERSONAL STORIES

"Everyone has something they can teach you."—Scott Bilker, 2001

Always Check Into Debt Consolidation Organizations

This section submitted by Christine, a DebtSmart® subscriber

My story begins like most of the people in this country. My husband and I had a lot of credit card debt that was getting out of control. We made some foolish decisions at a young age and were at this point suffering the consequences.

No matter how hard we tried, the debt just seemed to never go away. One day we decided to do some research on Consumer Credit Counseling Services. At the time, they were the only organization that was recommended for debt consolidation.

This seemed like our only hope because we wanted to purchase a house in the future. After doing our research, we decided to speak with one of the counselors and sign up for their program. Everything sounded wonderful. They actually advised us that creditors would review our credit report in a more positive fashion since we were now affiliated with CCCS.

Unfortunately that was not the case. Every month we made our scheduled payment on time and our debt was beginning to diminish. About 18 months later we decided to look into purchasing a home.

When we applied for the mortgage, to our surprise the mortgage company advised us that being member of CCCS was a step above bankruptcy. This was just like receiving a kick in the head. What happened to the positive aspects of being members of CCCS.

We were no where near bankruptcy. This was just a stepping stone to help us get out of debt. We weren't receiving harassing phone calls or collection notices. Now we were being marked as a bad risk. This was devastating.

I immediately contacted CCCS and to my surprise found out that our counselor was no longer affiliated with that office. We immediately spoke with another counselor and explained to them what was told to us. They were not helpful in any way. At that point I decided to take matters into my own hands. I wrote a very harsh letter to CCCS discontinuing our association with their organization.

Then my husband and I sat down and calculated what needed to be paid off and in how long a period of time. We then started examining our credit reports to see what negative information was on there and how we could repair them.

After a year we were able to pay off our debt (on our own) repair some of the negative information on our reports and purchase our first home. So we were able to turn a horrible situation into a happy one.

If it wasn't for that customer service representative at the mortgage company, we would have never know what a terrible impact CCCS could have done for our future credit history.

A word to the wise, always check into debt consolidation organizations very carefully and inquire with the credit report agencies what effect a debt consolidation agency may have on your future credit.

If it is your only hope, then become involved with a debt consolidation organization. But be aware that if they make promises to change your credit history from negative to positive, then they are frauds.

This is just a small piece of my continuing saga with credit.

How to Punish Your Credit-Card Bank

Has your credit-card bank ever made you angry? I mean really infuriated to the point where you just want a little revenge for how you were treated? The only problem is that you may feel at their mercy... like they're somehow superior. Well, you know what? They're not! No single bank has a monopoly on that "green paper" called money, and it's time to show them that if they don't treat you like the good customer you are, you're going to take your business elsewhere—in a big way. This point is well illustrated in a recent incident from my own personal consumer-credit experience.

I received an excellent credit offer from one of my credit cards that included a low rate for purchases. To maximize this offer, I needed to use the entire credit line by the offer's deadline. With at least $300 remaining in available credit, and being in need of a new 27-inch TV, I decided to take advantage of a sale at a local discount store.

The TV, with tax, came to $318. When the clerk swiped my credit card through the register, the transaction was rejected. I knew I was close to the limit, but since I'm into this credit stuff (I like to play these games for fun), I told the clerk to wait while I gave the bank a call. I wanted the bank to approve a credit-line increase on the spot so I could complete the transaction.

I called the customer-service phone number on the back of my card and spoke to an account rep, who transferred me to the credit department. I explained the situation and was told that I must give them some information before they could give me the increase. This translated into a formal phone application in which I had to disclose every single detail of my financial life to get "quick" approval.

After about one minute they came back with a NO response! I asked the woman, "Are you kidding? Why?" The reason: "Too many open accounts and too much debt." I told her to look at my payment record. She said, "You've never been late." Okay, now how about my record at your bank? Again, "Never late." In other words, I've charged and repaid more than $20,000, on time, over the last two years. "That's a lot of profit for your bank, and now you tell me that the first time I call and ask for help I can't even get a $50 credit-line increase?"

Her response was, "It's not bad [what the credit report says], I even asked the supervisor, and he said it's out of our hands. Sorry we couldn't help." To which I responded, "That's okay; I'm sure another bank CAN help." I also told her to note in my account record that "I'll be paying off my balance tomorrow so I'm not such a credit risk for the bank!"

Boy, was I fuming. I had to run to a MAC machine (ATM) to get cash for the TV purchase. My twenty-something clerk said, "Dude, that happened to me last week." Yeah, thanks for the credit advice, bro.

The next day I called another bank on my good-credit-offers list and had them issue a check to the offending bank—in full. That should get their attention. Their profit ends TODAY, but this story doesn't end here.

Like a movie with a good ending, I got to rub it in the bank's face. Eleven days later I get a call from that offending bank. Would you believe, they were offering a deal of 5.9% for six months plus no annual fee (like I'd really pay one anyway) if I stopped the balance transfer. Seems they received my transfer check and wanted me to void the check to keep my business in return for this so-called offer. I was gleaming! They had felt the pain of losing a good customer, and it hurt.

I asked the woman making this offer if she could see what had been going on in my account—particularly that I requested a credit-line increase and was refused. I explained that when I called and asked for help, they weren't there for me. I said, "I can't believe that after all the money I've charged and repaid on time, I am still considered a bad credit risk by this bank."

According to my notes, from charges and interest they were making about $900 a year from my account—and that number just went to zero. With all that profit and my perfect on-time record, the bank rejected my credit-line increase, forcing me to drive to an ATM and return so I could buy the TV. Then I had to turn to another bank to serve my credit needs because this bank doesn't know how to treat its customers.

I thanked the woman for listening and asked her to note in my account what I had said. I also told her that I will accept another offer from this bank sometime in the future—giving them another chance. I have plenty of good offers to choose from, and I don't need theirs, even though I would normally take it. I explained that I needed to punish them financially like they punished me while I was making a purchase.

The moral of this story, from the credit consumer's point of view, is that you need to have a good credit history to be able to punish a bank. You need to have other available credit lines to turn to in these situations. Let your banks know that you have many credit cards to choose from and that if you're not treated with the respect you deserve, you'll drop them in a heartbeat and go to another bank that wants to make a profit.

Identity Theft—A Personal Story
This section submitted by Robert B. Gamble

Several weeks ago I received a bill from Target Credit. I knew I did not apply for such a card, so I called the number related to the $160 worth of items charged and listed on the bill. They told me the items were shipped to someone in New York. Well, I was not about to pay for something I did not order, or receive, and I was not about to pay for a credit card that I did not even apply for.

I called Target, and came to find out that someone had signed up for the card, they had my name, my social security number, and my address, however the address had the wrong street number.

Needless to write, I told them to cancel the card and I filed a fraud report. Three months later, I am still receiving evidence that the thieves are still trying to use the card. Target assures me that they have canceled the card, and are not accepting any more charges. They assure me that their fraud department is handling it.

Thank you (Scott) for my Capital One card. Last week, I received a call from Capital One to verify if I truly wanted another Capital One Card. They noticed that the new application was to some address in West Virginia, and they wanted to confirm that I wanted the new card.

They provided Capital One my name, and my SSN and the new address. I told them no, and they told me I should contact the three different credit report companies and put a statement in that would require the credit report companies to contact me when any new credit cards are applied for. Kathy (the Capital One person) gave me the phone numbers for the three credit report companies and suggested I call them ASAP.

As soon as I hung up, I called them. The three companies are:
- Experian (888) 397-3742
- Trans Union (800) 680-7289
- EquiFax, Phone # from the Credit Report - (866) 233-3780
  Address: Equifax Information Services, P.O. Box 740256, Atlanta, GA 30374-0256. Could not speak to anyone: (800) 685-1111 or (800) 270-3435 or, for online help: (888) 532-0179 Fax machine number: (888) 729-0083

I was able to contact Experian & Trans Union and speak to a live person. They helped me file the necessary information, and said I would receive a letter within 10 days. EquiFax, only has an automated number which wants to charge $39.95 a month for their protection service.

I have not contacted the number from the credit report that I received last month (Just by chance I ordered a Free report which came from EquiFax). While the credit report does not show the Target card, or any other card I don't know about, I still want to call and file the fraud report to require contacting me before issuing any new cards.

I hope this helps you and your readers, and again thanks for the Capital One card.

Manipulating the System

It's Friday night and the phone rings... you know the call, it's late, the last bite of my dinner being chewed, all you want to do is watch TV and relax. Guess who's calling? Yes, it's a mortgage company that's trying to sell me a refinance deal!

The girl asks me about my mortgage, my rates, and my credit card debts. To which I do reply, after all I'm always curious about getting a better loan (plus I love toying with these people).

I ask her what their best rates are. She tells me that it depends on my credit history. I said, "Okay, say I have a credit rating like Bill Gates. NOW what's your best rate?" She said that she can't quote a rate however, the loan officer would let me know. So I agreed to have the loan officer give me a call.

On Monday, while I'm trying to set up the new DVD player, the phone rings. Guess who? It's the loan officer, let's just call him Kevin. Well okay, so Kevin is really his name. I'm not going to change names to protect the innocent. ☺

Kevin starts his spiel about how he can save me money on my $110,000 30-year, 6 7/8% mortgage and $15,000 of credit card debt. I asked him what his best rates are and he told me it varied depending on my credit score, which he could check if I tell him my social security number—I don't think so! There's no way I'm giving that out over the phone. If his deal sounds real then I'll ask for paperwork to be sent through the mail.

I told him to assume that "My credit history is the best of anyone on earth and in this universe. Now, what is your best rate?" He told me 6.5% with 1 point.

He went on to explain that unlike other mortgage companies that ask for the 1 point at closing, they "conveniently" include that amount in the mortgage principal. I told him that 6.5%

isn't that much better than my 6 7/8% (6.875%) and when you throw in the 1 point then your "best" loan is really around 6.6%.

That's when he asked me what my credit card rates are. I told him that my credit card debts are at about 1.99% APR, which are a little high since I had the entire $15,000 at 0% for the prior 20 months.

Kevin said that I'm really not getting 1.99% and that there's no way I ever got 0%. He said, "Tell me where I can get those credit card rates?"

I told him to look in his mailbox. That's where many great credit card deals are found. And most really good ones are offered from your current banks.

He still didn't believe me and said that if I look at my statement I'd see that I was really paying 16% or more. I explained that when I had those 0% deals, my credit card statement would arrive and show a balance of $15,000 and under "finance charges" the total is "$0.00."

His response was, "Think about it, Scott...why would a bank give you 0%. They're not making any money!"

I said, "To get new customers."

Kevin then told me that it doesn't make sense that they would do that. I said, "Well then, does it make sense that Publisher's Clearing House gives away $10 million, or that McDonalds gives away millions in prizes? Why do they do it? To get business."

Why do the banks offer 0%? Because they think that I'm going to forget that the offer ended and let my rate bounce to 15% (or more). I'm not!

I'm simply going to transfer my balance to another low-rate offer when their offer ends. Overall, the bank will make money because most people (not DebtSmart® readers—we're all too "debt smart") are not going to not notice that the rates have been increased or will be too lazy to continue transferring balances.

After I told Kevin how I keep transferring my balances he said pretentiously, "*So you're manipulating the system.*"

I said, "I'm taking advantage of my best loan options. You just called me and are trying to get me to transfer my mortgage and credit card debt to your bank. If I decide to use your offer, am I then 'manipulating the system'?"

That comment really caused Kevin's brain to freeze up. Almost as locked-up as Windows 98 with 20 open applications. He was forced to shut down and restart.

He finally replied with, "Well no."

"So then, if I use other bank's offers I'm 'manipulating the system' but if I use your offer then I'm not. Is that right?"

Kevin said, "Well I guess you're just being smart."

You see my friends, there is a stigma about transferring balances. People say that you're "credit surfing," that you're "manipulating the system" or "using Peter to pay Paul" (I don't owe Paul anything) or "paying one credit card with another."

Hear me on this...DON'T listen to these myths. Don't be brainwashed by this dogma! It's always DebtSmart® to use your best loan options! It's doesn't matter how many times you switch cards. You're always going to save money when you pick a better loan deal.

Kevin changed the subject by trying to give me numbers for his refinancing deal. He said that my payments, with his 6.5%, 30-year, mortgage for my $110,000 would be about $750.00 per month. Of course I always have my calculator handy and I told him that the payments are more like $695.28, in fact, they are exactly $695.28. He said that he's including his 1 point fee in the payment.

Well then, according to my numbers the payment is $702.23. I asked him how he's coming up with $750. Kevin said, "It's obvious that you have a calculator there."

My response was "Yeah, I have a calculator here. What do you have there? Whatever you have doesn't seem to be able to come up with the correct payment."

Finally, since he can't talk about facts anymore he starts to get emotional and says, "Look, I've been doing this for years. I do this all day. What do you do over there at Press One?"

"I write and publish books, I run a web site, write an email newsletter." However, I never did mention to Kevin the subject matter.

Lastly, I should say that Kevin was nice and I do want to thank him for calling because it resulted in this informative article.

CHAPTER 4

CARS

"If it's the radiator or a hose, it's the radiator."—Scott Bilker, 1997

Consider Financing Your Next Car with a Credit Card

Buy a car with a credit card! Sound crazy? Well, just hear me out on this one.

Before we get started there are a few words of caution that need mentioning. Specifically, if you can afford to buy a car with cash, that's your best option. Any time you use your credit cards you run the risk of getting further into debt. But I would be doing you a disservice if I didn't let you know about yet another way you can save money!

I'm going to discuss five reasons why you need to consider your credit cards when financing a car.

First, when you use a credit card, the loan is unsecured. That means that if for some reason you have financial problems in the future, your car is not in jeopardy of being repossessed. You own it outright. The bank can't visit you in the middle of the night and drive it away.

Second, you always have the option of paying less per month. When financing a car people tend to want to pay off the loan within three to four years. Of course, the shorter the loan, the greater the monthly payment. If financing is obtained from a bank, the monthly payments are fixed for the loan term. But what happens if after couple months you a have difficult time coming up with the full monthly payment? If you're late or don't pay in full you could potentially damage your credit history. Now if you use a credit card to finance the car, you can make payments that retire the loan in three years but if you have any problems in any given month, you have the option to make the minimum payment, which would be considerably less.

Third, you don't have to wait for a loan approval. You can just use your credit line like cash anytime you're ready to buy. No need to go into the back room with the car salesman to start talking about loan rates and loan applications.

Fourth, because you're using a credit line, preferably a check, you have more bargaining power when you're making the car purchase. From the car dealer standpoint, you're buying the car with your own money. That means you don't have to deal with the secondary transaction of getting the loan. You can essentially say, "See this check, give me the deal I want, and I'll fill in the numbers right now."

Fifth and most importantly, you can save big money! When you finance anything-car, house, last night's dinner-you are really making two purchases. The first is the actual object you want to acquire-the car. The second is the money you are using to make the first purchase.

Each of these transactions needs to be carefully considered if you want to ensure that you receive the best deal. Assuming that you did the best possible job at negotiating a reasonable price for the car, we're going to move on to the purchase of the money, or the financing.

When you considered the value of the car, you had to compare it to other vehicles and their various features-power brakes, air bags, etc. Each car is different and you must weigh those differences carefully when deciding how much you are willing to pay for the car. But when it comes to the purchase of the money (the loan), every banks' cash is the same.

Here's a description of the product you get from the bank.. green paper called money. It's all the same no matter which bank you borrow it from. It doesn't matter if the money comes from dealer financing, a bank loan, credit card, a second mortgage, or your neighbor. The only consideration when comparing each loan is its cost. How much will you end up paying for the use of that money today.

Let's say you're buying a used car and still need to finance $9,500. Used car loan interest rates range from 6.95% to 16.63% with the average being 9.95%. After visiting many banks, you may discover that your best rate, for whatever reason, is 10%. But you also have an offer from one of your credit cards for 4.9% for six months, and you have more than $9,500 in available credit. Is it worth using the card? You bet! At least for six months.

The bank loan at 10% APR, $9500 for three years gives you a monthly payment of $306.54. After paying the loan for six months, you'll still owe $8107.02. Now, the correct question to ask yourself is how much would you owe in six months if you use the credit-card offer and make payments of $306.54? The answer is $7877.02. That means you saved $230 by using the credit card for six months.

Some people may say, "So what, 230 bucks, big deal." Fine then, go straight to the nearest bank and make a donation of $230 to the bank manager...doesn't feel too good does it? What happened to "a penny saved is a penny earned"? If you could have gotten another $230 off the price of the car from the dealer, you'd be very happy with yourself. My point is that you can find better things to do with the $230 saved.. like pay back other debts.

At the end of the six-month credit-card offer, the rate will probably go up, so you'll need to re-examine your financing at that time. You can always go to the first bank that offered you 10% and ask for a secured loan at that time to pay off the credit-card balance. But the bottom line is that you are locking in the $230 savings.

Don't finance your car blindly. Consider all your options carefully and you'll get the best deals and save a lot of money.

Excerpt from *Credit Card and Debt Management*
Chapter 5 (Math and Money)

My father asked me to help him pick out a new car. After visiting several new car dealers in the area we finally found one with a car that had the price and features we were looking for. Once the negotiations were complete, and the price was agreed upon, it was time for the dealership to add in those extras such as; tags, processing fees and anything else they could.

Finally, the balance due for the car was presented and we decided to finance it. The salesman told me the length of the loan and the interest rate. I already knew the amount to be financed so it was easy to calculate the monthly payments. It was at this time that we were instructed to go into a separate office to read and sign the loan agreement. When the contract came out of the computer the monthly payment shown was $65 a month higher than I had calculated! That $65 per month for entire length of the 5-year loan would total $3,900! I expressed my concern and was told that, "you can't figure out monthly payments with a simple calculator" and "the computer is right." I informed the salesman that unless the payments were what I computed, the deal was off and I would be visiting the dealer across the street who would be happy to have my business. Furthermore, I was using a scientific calculator which can easily handle simple monthly payment problems.

Once they saw I was serious, it was explained that the computer "accidentally" added a charge on for an extended warranty and undercoating. They adjusted for this error that they "obviously had no idea occurred," and told me the new payment. This time it was closer, but still off by $10 a month. This might not seem like much money but $10 a month for 60 months is $600 and I would rather keep the $600 than contribute it to the next dealership rob-the-customer-day party. I told them again that they were wrong and I was not going to allow my father to sign any agreement until the numbers were correct!

After searching, they finally "discovered" what went wrong. Another computer blip that they had no control over. It turned out that the interest rate on the agreement was not the one they originally quoted me. Once all the numbers were correct the computer spit out the correct monthly payment and we got the car.

I am not trying to imply the dealership tried to rip me off. Oh, no! But what is certainly true is that if I did not know how much the payment was supposed to be, my father might have signed that agreement and paid a huge unnecessary fee.

Since then I have helped many of my friends buy cars. In each case, the starting monthly payment was always higher than I calculated and later reduced to the correct number. These are real examples of the necessity of being able to solve simple math problems.

Car Dealers

Question

Scott,

I know that you have used these examples to help people learn and to be aware but you have also just made every car dealer in the country a crook.

I grew up in a family that owns car dealerships and have been working here for a number of years. I have been in the finance and insurance office for 3 1/2 years and have never quoted insurance or extended service plans in a final payment without first explaining what it is and letting a customer decide the type of plan they want.

Secondly, because of disclosure laws, your father and friends would have had to sign separate forms for credit life, disability, and extended service plans giving them yet another opportunity to change their minds, and yet a third opportunity exists. You can cancel any one of those plans within a time period without any financial obligation.

Now, I'm not saying there aren't dealers out there doing exactly what you experienced and I'd never tell a car buyer to not be aware, but I think people should go looking for an honest dealership that exists on its integrity rather than to force a bad dealership to comply.

By giving the corrupt dealership your business, even if you get them to comply, still allows them to make money and stay in business.

—Heather

Answer

Heather,

Personally, I have yet to buy a car from a dealer that I considered being "totally" honest. Every situation I've been involved in, when buying a new or used car, has resulted in some type of attempt to get me to pay more.

You mention how people have to sign separate forms for credit, extended service plan, etc. However, it doesn't matter what extra papers you sign if you don't know what they mean or their true costs.

In my father's case, without my being there, he would have signed any documents they gave him! Sure, he has 72 hours to back out of the deal but it doesn't matter because he never would have reviewed the details.

I once attended a class in negotiation. The instructor told the class that when you enter negotiations you should always tell the truth, with one exception, when you're buying a car. He went on to tell us that his close personal friend is a car dealer and revealed many sales "techniques."

One "technique" he revealed was quite interesting. They actually bugged the desks where the customers worked with the salespeople. This way, if for example, a husband and wife were ironing out the final details of the purchase, the dealer could listen in on their conversation when the salesperson left the area.

I actually had a feeling this was happening one time when I was buying a car. The salesperson I was working with knew a lot about my thinking that day—coincidence, I don't think so!

My advice to everyone is that when you're negotiating for the price of a car, and the salesperson leaves the desk, turn to your friend and say, "If this salesman doesn't give me the car for $X then let's go down the street to the next dealer." Keep up the act even when nobody is there because you don't know who's listening.

Then, when you go in the back room for financing, it's round two for "some" dishonest dealers to take advantage. In fact, in October 2000, 20/20, did piece called "The Car Dealer's Secret."

In this segment they investigated how some dealers would mark up interest rates by huge amounts!

This is how it happens. Car dealers don't know the rate you're qualified to receive. They submit your application to lenders who approve you for a certain interest rate. Then the dealer marks up the rate and splits the profit with the lender!

It gets worse. 20/20 also reported that there was evidence that black customers were twice as likely as whites to have their rates marked up!

So you see, I'd love to give my business to a "non-corrupt" dealer. I'm sure that there are honest dealers out there, but the problem is that I haven't found one yet and by the time I find out that they are dishonest, it's too late.

—Scott

Q&A: Buy a Car with a Cash Advance?

Question

Hi Scott,
Read your article Consider Financing Your Next Car with a Credit Card and as you asked I'm commenting on same. The logic of the 4.9% at 6 Months makes sense, BUT is it a reality? You said use your credit, WRITE A CHECK, isn't writing a check tantamount to a CASH ADVANCE? I believe it is with most credit card companies. If it is, then aren't you looking at a much higher interest rate? Example, one of my credit cards has PURCHASES @ 18.90, while CASH ADVANCES are at 23.00! And, any monies paid against the balance ALWAYS goes to the lower interest rate! Any comment? BTW, I enjoyed the article and you have a great website! Very interesting, informative & helpful "stuff!"
—Mel

Answer

Mel,

Thank you for writing!

You're correct that you would probably have to write a check. And yes, it's a cash advance, however, I have many, many, many, no-fee, low rate, check offers. I have one I just used for 2.99%, no-fees, which is far better than any used car loan I could get otherwise.

I said in my article to "consider" using your credit card. If it doesn't make sense in your case, then don't do it, but many people may be able to get a better deal this way.

Talk to you later.

—Scott

Reply

I just wanted to see if my train of thought process with regard to interest rates (cash vs purchase) was correct. BTW, know where I can get a credit card with a $75,000 credit line, I want to buy a used Ferrari! Keep up the great work, love your website!
—Mel

Q&A: Car Debt or Credit Debt First?

Question

Scott,
First off great site, very informative.
I've already organized my debt with the highest interest debt to be paid off first. Only thing is, my car loan is up toward the top and it's getting close to the time when I would need to roll over the payments of paid off debt to the next highest interest rate debt, my car loan.
Does it make sense to start increasing my payments on this loan? Isn't it fixed what I will pay on the loan? If this is the case shouldn't I start paying on the next highest interest debt (another credit card) instead? Thanks for any help!
—Mike

Answer

Mike,

Thanks your positive comments about DebtSmart®!

It's great that you've already set up a payment program that pays the highest-interest-rate debts back first. Many financial "experts" advise to pay off the lowest-balance debt first but that's simply wrong, meaning, more expensive!

Since your car loan is about to become the most expensive debt, highest interest rate, you should "roll" your payments from the last debt into the car loan. This is the most efficient method of repaying your debt.

There are however, a few details you need to check:

1) Are you allowed to pay off your car loan early with larger payments? There are some loans that have pre-payment penalty conditions so call the bank to make sure you can send in more money toward the loan principal.

2) When you send in your payments be sure the bank knows to apply the entire payment toward your balance. There are a few instances when the bank will apply the scheduled payment and hold the extra for the next payment. You don't want that situation.

3) Will you need that extra cash in the near future? If you pay more toward a credit card you can always get that cash back if you need it by using a cash advance or making purchases with the card. When you increase the payment on the car, that money becomes part of the car and cannot be converted back into cash again until the car is sold.

In summary, you are correct. It makes perfect sense to send the extra payment to the car loan because it's the most expensive debt on your list. Just be sure there are no penalties for paying off the loan early. If there are penalties, you'll need to consider if the savings from the interest charges are greater than penalties. Chances are you can pay off the loan early; if there are penalties let me know.

Keep up the good work!

—Scott

DON'T GET RIPPED OFF

"Being DebtSmart® means being able to uncover the true costs of all your credit options"
—Scott Bilker, 2001

Reading the Fine Print in those Low-Rate Credit Card Offers

Taking advantage of low-rate offers is almost always a good idea. That's where the bulk of interest savings are found when you're managing your debt. However, there may be hidden costs that need to be uncovered before deciding to accept a seemingly good deal. It is imperative that you read through and understand the entire low-rate offer. That includes the letter, the back of the letter, and every bit of the fine print.

I want to talk about the details you can expect to find in those low-rate credit card offers letters. The conditions that you need to consider to ensure you're going to get the better end of this offer. They are the details I always look at and note before jumping into any credit offer.

First: The most important factor is the interest rate, which can usually be found in big bold letters on the envelope in which the offer was received. This should make it stand out from most of the usual junk that fills the mailbox. The best offers will probably be found with your existing creditors. They may be trying to encourage you to do some business with them or attempting to get you to transfer your balance from another credit card.

In order to save money with a balance transfer, you must be sure you are switching from a rate that is currently higher than the new offer. There are, of course, other considerations to keep in mind that we'll be discussing soon, but in general, if this condition is not true, you won't be able to save any money.

Second: What I call the time-to-act date. This is the latest day you can take advantage of the offer. I've noticed lately that there can be other conditions related to this date. Specifically, different rates for different acting dates. For example, "if you act by this date the rate is 8.9%, if you wait until two weeks later the rate is 9.9%, and finally one month later the rate is 10.9%."

Third: Length of time the new low rate will be applied to your account. This time can vary from three months to a year and can make a big difference in how much you save. The longer the time you're in the new lower rate, the more money you save. That's obvious, but there is certainly a break-even time when compared to your current rate. In other words, if fees are included as a condition of the transfers, you'll have to be in the lower rate for a certain amount of time before you start seeing any savings.

Fourth: How the payments are applied. If you have an existing balance on the credit line in which you're getting the new offer, you have to be careful of how payments get applied to your account. For example, you may have purchases at 14.9% in the amount of $1,000. The new offer is for 6.9%, but your payments will be applied to your last transaction. This means that if you transfer $2,000 at 6.9% and make a payment of $100, the entire $100 is applied to the 6.9% transfer amount. This is great for the bank since your balance of $1,000 still has interest accruing at 14.9% until you are finished paying back the transfer amount.

Fifth: The amount you're allowed to transfer. This one can be tricky. Most offers allow you to "transfer up to your credit limit" which is fine. That's the best option. However, they often don't specify exactly how much you can transfer. It's tricky because you might go over your credit limit when you include fees and interest charges. For example, you have a $2,000 credit line and an offer to transfer balances at 5.9%. There's a 2% transfer fee and no grace period on balance transfers. What happens when you transfer $2,000?

Well the 2% transfer fee is $40 bringing the total to $2,040. Then one month of interest on the new balance at 5.9% is $10, which brings the balance to $2,050. Oops, over the limit, now you're getting hit with a $25 over-limit fee bringing the total to $2,075. So, when the smoke clears, you paid $75 in fees for one month on a $2,000 balance—that's equivalent to an APR of 45%!

This is a topic you may need to discuss with an account rep to make sure you don't break any rules. If you go over your limit, you will be hit with a penalty. Here's Scott's rule on penalties and fees, "If the bank can charge you a fee—it will."

Sixth: Fees that may be imposed on the balance transfer. I think you'll find that most balance transfer offers will not impose any transfer fees. To make sure, you must read carefully or it can cost you big-time. There are, however, times you will be forced to pay a transfer fee, which is based on the amount transferred, if you want to get the low rate. This fee can be very high. It is usually based on either: (1) some minimum amount like $2 no matter the amount of the transfer, (2) 2% of the amount transferred, or (3) a maximum charge (ceiling)—like $20. But there are some banks that have no ceiling on the amount of the fee. So if you transfer $7,000 with a 2% fee, the total fee comes out to $140. It may still be worthwhile to use an offer like this, but you must know if, when compared to what you're currently paying, you're saving money.

Seventh: Is there a grace period for transfers? A grace period is a set amount of time in which your account balance will not be charged interest. It is very rare indeed to get a low-rate that doesn't charge you money when you transfer your balance. It does happen sometimes, and that can be a great bonus! On one occasion I was able to transfer $5,000 from 8.9% to 3.9% and was allowed a one-month interest-free period on that transfer. The instant savings amounted to $37 because that's what it would have cost to leave it at 8.9% for the month. Not to worry if there is no grace period because it is only fair that interest is charged from the instant you take the loan. This is, after all, how mortgages work.

Eighth: Late payment conditions. This is where you must be extremely careful. Your low-rate offer could evaporate into thin air and end up costing you hundreds of extra dollars if you do not meticulously read all of the conditions. This condition is always in the real superfine print and usually goes something like, "However, if a minimum monthly payment is not received by the close of the first full billing cycle following its Payment Due Date, your promotional APR balances will be 24.9%." That's a big increase from the 3.9% in the offer, and that's just for being late once! The bottom line here is that if you do decide to take advantage of the offer, you must be vigilant at making sure your payments are on time.

Ninth: How is the transfer to be conducted? There are three popular methods: (1) a fill-in-the-blank transfer sheet you return to the bank with their business reply envelope, (2) balance-transfer checks, and (3) call the bank. I have seen cases where there are transfer fees imposed when you use the balance-transfer checks. However, if you call and ask about that fee, you may find that it is waived completely if you do the transfer by phone with an account representative. Obviously, the no-fee choice is superior. Again, these details should be in your letter, on the back of the letter, or included on the checks themselves. It may not state that it's free if you call and transfer balances by phone. So if there is a fee imposed, call and find out if it can be waived.

Tenth: Different rates for different amounts transferred. This type of information might be found in the large-print section of the letter but then again, maybe not. It works like this—the more you transfer the lower the rate. For example, "0 to $2,999 is at 8.9%, $3,000 to $4,999 is at 7.9%, over $5,000 is at 6.9%." This is very important in calculating how much you can save. Obviously, the lower the rate the better.

Eleventh: Any annual fees? If the low-rate offer is conditional on your applying for a new line of credit, you'll need to consider the cost of the account itself. Again, it may turn out that even if there is an annual fee, you may be better off with the new card. Annual fees can run very high, maybe as much as $50, so make sure that it is clearly stated whether or not there is an annual fee and if so, its amount.

Twelfth: What the rate will go to when the promotion is over. Hopefully, for the bank's sake, they're going to raise the rate to a fair level, but I've seen offers that end with rates going to near 20%! That's just too high for me and it's too high for you. You need to know the rate when the promotion ends to more accurately calculate how much your savings will total. That is, assuming that you're not going to switch to a new offer. What happens in reality is that before the time runs out for one promotion, you'll have many others to choose from—that's why I say, "for the bank's sake" because you'll be gone if they try to gouge you.

Let's look at an example and see if a balance transfer is worth doing. Here's the situation. You currently owe $2,000 to a credit card with an 11.9% APR. You're paying $100 per month toward that debt which, at that rate, will be paid off in 23 months (1 year, 11 months) and cost a total of $2,240.35.

There are two balance transfer options available to consider:

Option 1: Interest rate is 3.9% APR for one year, then it jumps to 9.9% for the next year. There is a 3% cash advance fee for transfers and a $50 annual fee.

Option 2: Interest rate is 4.9% APR for 6 months, then it jumps to 10.9% and there's an annual fee of $15.

Option 3: Don't forget, you can do nothing and stay at 11.9%.

Which of your three options is better?

It turns out that option 1 actually costs more than doing nothing! After the loan is repaid, this option ends up costing $2,271.81, which is $31.46 over the repayment amount if you don't do the transfer in the first place. Notice how enticing it sounds though—3.9% for one year. That's why you have to do the math! As it turns out, the true APR for this offer is 13.22%.

Looking at option 2, the total repaid is $2,188.29! Now that's an offer worth doing a transfer on because it's $52.06 better than staying at the 11.9%, not to mention $83.52 better than option 1. The true APR for option 2 is 9.61%, clearly the winner. I'll be talking about how to figure out those numbers in future articles. A nice exercise would be for you to give that a try and see how you do.

Anyway, there are those who would say, "Scott, that's a lot of work for only $52.06. You gotta make all those comparisons, fill out paperwork, etc. It's not worth it." Well, for those people who don't feel it's worth saving 52 bucks, please write me a check in that amount today since it's not much. I doubt I'll have any takers.

The trick to these offers is the fancy way the numbers are presented. For example, say you're at a department store and there's a sale with an offer of, "take 25% off retail and then take another 25% off!" Sounds almost like taking 50%-right? Let's see, if an item is $100 then the first 25% off brings the price to $75, but the next 25% is based on $75 which is $18.75 so the total price becomes $56.25. The real discount total is 43.75%.

Lastly, since the marketing of these promotions is always changing, you have to stay on top of all your offers and read all new offers very carefully. In the end, it's your responsibility to get the best deal—caveat emptor.

One day late, yeah right!

I knew it, I knew it, I knew it!

A couple years ago most credit card banks changed their policy of what "late" means to meaning "one day late is late." It used to be that late was if your payment was due on the 1st but received on, say, the 20th. Not anymore. If you're 24 hours late, it's late, and you will be charged the late fee. Late fees have also been rising and some are now as high as $35!

What did I know?

I had the feeling that since being one day late means that banks can charge a late fee, it's possible that, well, payments could "accidentally" be held for say, oh, 24 hours. Oops, you're late!

My theory was a step closer to confirmation when one of my credit card payments was exactly one day late. I always track everything—every check, every payment date, and all transactions. I use Quicken and other custom software I developed to pay my bills. So when I was late by one day I took a look at the date that bank's check was mailed.

Guess how early I mailed the payment?

Seven days!

The 8th day was the late day. I called the bank and told them that they'd better waive that fee or I would transfer my balance and close the account. They did waive the fee for me, but I wonder how many other people don't call to waive these one-day-late fees?

I wonder how many people simply pay the late fee because they figure "I was late." Being exactly one day late has happened to many people I know. I asked them if they called the bank to complain and they said that they didn't because they thought they were actually late.

Tell you what, being one day late isn't worth 35 bucks! There is no way that it costs the bank $35 for someone to be one day late.

The way I see it is that it's like being mugged in an alley!

As it turns out my theory is even closer to confirmation. Look at those small slips of paper with fine print that come with your statement. Many of those papers are lawsuit notifications from banks that are accused of "not crediting payments promptly," and charging late fees.

The funny thing is that in these class action lawsuits, when the smoke clears, the lawyers get paid millions and most of us only get back a few cents! Every case that I'm involved in, because I'm a cardholder, has been settled without the bank having to admit any wrongdoing.

What can we do?

Be sure to look at every charge on your credit card statement. Don't let the bank get away with charging you a late fee. I don't care if it's really your fault for being late!

First of all, it doesn't matter because $35 is a rip-off for being 24 hours late. And, second of all, the bank should treat you like gold for being a good customer, and should waive at least one late fee as a courtesy even if it IS your fault.

Giving Up Your Rights—Without Knowing It!

I received a letter from Capital One informing me that "enclosed is an important legal notice regarding arbitration" and I need to "read the entire notice to fully understand its implications" to my account.

This isn't the easiest reading by the way. It's a legal notice, written in legal language at the college graduate level. Quite different than the 6th-grade level credit offers they send me trying to get me to use my credit lines.

Here's an example from the arbitration letter: "The arbitration of any Claim must proceed on an individual basis, even if the Claim has been asserted in a court as a class action, private attorney general action or other representative of collective action."

Oh yeah, makes perfect sense to me.

Here's an example of the writing that's meant for me to easily understand (from a credit offer): "One of the attached Purchase Checks is already made payable to you. Consider using the other check to purchase something you've always wanted. It's that easy!"

Gee, I can understand that no problem. Why the difference in writing style? Could it be that in one case it's meant for me to be confused and in the other they want me to spend money on my credit lines? Could it be that both cases are written to work in Capital One's advantage? We both know the answers to those questions.

Here's the bottom line on this arbitration letter: if you do not reject the Arbitration Provision then it becomes part of your account. It's a "negative offer" similar to the music clubs that automatically send you the "CD of the Month" unless you tell them not to send it.

So what's the Arbitration Provision? It means that if you have a dispute that's listed in what they consider to be a dispute, the matter is taken to an impartial person, or group, to be resolved.

Of course, you can choose your arbitrator—from their list.

It means that if you allow this provision to become part of your agreement you will not have the right to take your claim to court or participate in a class action lawsuit. And it may cost MORE to go to arbitration, probably because your attorney's fee could be covered for many claims, like say a class action lawsuit.

You may ask why it's important retain these rights?

First of all, I don't want to give up any rights unnecessarily, but more importantly is that although we are only going to recover pennies in a class action lawsuit, it's still in our best interest to be a part of these cases. Sure, the lawyers get all the money, but these lawsuits are one of the best defenses to keep the banks in check. It reminds them that they need to obey the law or they'll pay!

Here is a list of some of what they'll consider a "claim" (dispute you have with them or they have with you):

- Transactions or attempted transactions on your account.
- Any billing or collection matters.
- Any fees, interest, or their calculation.
- Any products, services, or benefits programs in connection with your account (any insurance, rebates, rewards, etc.).
- Any posting of transactions (including payments and credit) to your account.

I called their contact number in the letter to ask questions but only connected to their recording system that delivers answers based on a phone menu. In others, words, I couldn't reach a human—no surprise there.

I would urge you to STOP the Arbitration Provision from becoming part of your credit card agreement! I don't see it as being in our favor at all!

Here's the general rule: When businesses spend money to send you an offer it's usually in their best interest and probably not yours. There are exceptions; however, I always approach all offers with a level of skepticism.

I have received term changes from other credit card banks which, if rejected, mean that the account is closed. The only consequence of rejecting the Arbitration Provision, which I saw in the letter, is that it doesn't become part of your account terms.

Let's look at this from Capital One's point of view. They're lending money to many people who are going to stiff them in bankruptcy court. I can understand why they need to protect themselves, however, they must treat us "DebtSmart®" customers with respect. We are their best clients, and we need to stick together to show all the banks who's really in control—who's paying their salaries!

Don't give up any of your rights!

Although I feel like they are trying to pull a fast one here I still like Capital One and recommend their credit card because the interest rates are generally lower than other credit cards. In their defense, on this Arbitration Policy change issue at least they indicated all the salient information in bold print on the envelope and in the letter.

Problems And Solutions: Loan Savings

Congratulations to Tiffiny who won the third contest offered in the DebtSmart® Email Newsletter! And congratulations to everyone as a group because 83% of the respondents had the correct answer!

QUESTION:

You have an outstanding credit card balance of $5,500 at 15.99% APR (fixed) and you're making payments of $99.87 per month. With those payments this loan will be paid off in exactly 100 months. You decide to save money by transferring this balance to an 9.99% APR (fixed) and keep making the same monthly payment of $99.87. The good news is that you can now pay off your loan in only 74 months! How much money do you save? Is it $2,596, $2,182, or $1,768?

SOLUTION:

$2,596, since the payment is kept constant, the total savings is equal to the number of payments not paid. It takes 100 payments to pay off the 15.99% loan and only 74 payments to pay off the 9.99% loan.

Therefore, you save 26 payments or 26 times $99.87, which is $2,596.62 when comparing the savings over a 100-month period.

It's important to recognize that you're really saving money THE ENTIRE TIME! The savings is relative to every point in time. In the problem I implied that you find the savings over the entire 100 month period, however, there are savings every month.

Let's compare both loans one month at a time. Before the first payment, each loan has an unpaid balance of $5,500. Total savings is zero. However, after the first payment is made, the balance remaining on the 15.99% loan is $5,473.42 and the balance for the 9.99% loan is $5,445.92. That means that you saved the difference, $25.50, after the first payment.

The 9.99% loan is paid off at payment number 74 which means its balance is zero. So what would you still owe on the 15.99% loan? That amount is $2,181.97.

From this point forward all the payments that would have been made to the 15.99% are saved because you have the 9.99% loan.

Problems And Solutions: Fuzzy Mortgage

This is a tricky question so please read through the entire answer. It's this type of "fuzzy math" that can end up costing people a bundle!

QUESTION: Which loan is better and why?

Loan 1: $100,000.00, 30-year loan, with monthly payments of $665.31. That's a total out-of-pocket cost of $665.31 x 360 months = $239,511.60.

Loan 2: $100,000.00, 15-year loan, with monthly payments of $1,014.27. That's a total out-of-pocket cost of $1,014.27 x 180 months = $182,568.60

SOLUTION: Loan 1 is better because it really does cost less!

Let's pretend that I already have loan 1. Now imagine having a mortgage broker trying to sell me loan 2 to replace my loan 1.

Here's the pitch. "Scott, listen, if you do a 15-year mortgage with the $1,014.27 monthly payment, you'll save $56,943.00! Just sign here!"

Is the broker lying? Well, not technically, however it is true that loan 2, even though it "seems" like it saves you money, is actually more expensive!

Even under the sales pressure I would go get my calculator to figure out the most important cost for any loan, the interest rate (APR).

It turns out that Loan 1 is 7% and Loan 2 is 9%. I used the DebtSmart® Loan Calculator to get the rates.

Armed with that information, I'd say to the mortgage broker, "Why would I want to use the 15-year, 9% loan over the 7% loan?" To which the response is, "Rate doesn't matter, you save $56,943.00! Scott, are you trying to tell me that you don't save $56,943.00, are you saying that I'm a liar!"

He's not lying. It's true that loan 2 does save $56,943.00 over loan 1.

So then, how is it better to use loan 1? How can loan 1 possibly be cheaper when it is true that loan 2 saves $56,943.00?

Fuzzy math!

It's an unfair math comparison. A trick question. It's not an apples-to-apples comparison because the monthly payments are not equal!

I would say to the broker. "Rate does matter. If I can afford to make a $1,014.27 monthly payment to loan 2 then I can afford to make the same payment to loan 1. When I do that I can pay off loan 1 in 12.27 years. Which is obviously much shorter than the 15-year option. In fact, if I did that I can pay off loan 1 with a total of $149,341.11. That pay off figure is $33,227.49 cheaper than the 15-year option!"

At that point the mortgage broker would either act confused, because he doesn't get it, or look surprised that you figured out his fuzzy-math game.

The main key to comparing loans is being sure that the comparison is fair. That means that you can only have one parameter change and all others held constant. To make a fair comparison in this case the principal ($100,000) and payments must remain the same for both situations. The change is in the rate (7% or 9%). Keep in mind that the repayment-times change however, it's because the repayment-time is a function of the principal, rate, and payment.

Once we make the fair comparison, it's clear that loan 1 is the better, cheaper loan.

Quick mention...many people did respond and say that loan 1 was better because you can use the difference between the payment for investment purposes.

Of course, you need to know the interest rates before doing the investing since to make the investment worthwhile you'd need to make the same rate as the loan cost just to break even. However, thinking about "using the difference between the payments" is a clear sign that there's extra money floating around. That extra money is a symptom of the "fuzzy math".

CHAPTER 6

PLANNING, PAYING, AND SAVING

"Your DebtSmart® plan is your roadmap to financial success!"—Scott Bilker, 2002

Q&A: Scott, you have too many credit cards!

Question

Scott,

I read your article in which you state that you have 80 or so credit cards. I'm not sure why this is advantageous. I have cancelled all but one card which I pay in full each month and by no means see my "options" (to get into debt, I guess) as being restricted.

For instance, I did need to carry a balance for 3 months to pay for an engagement ring at the beginning of this year. All I did was charge it to my everyday card, which has a lousy rate but gives me perks, get a new card with a low rate so I paid almost no interest for those three months, then closed that card when it was paid. This is actually better than calling the banks for the best rate because the cards with the perks almost always have the lousy rates, so you're better off putting it onto one of those cards, and then transferring it to a lower rate card, then you get the perks.

The problem with having multiple cards that go unused is that potential creditors will count available credit against you when you apply for a mortgage or a car.

Also, the more open accounts you have, the greater the chance of being defrauded. Having only one card is by no means restrictive there are hundreds of companies who would give me a card after a 5-minute phone call. I just don't see the point in keeping cards that aren't being used open
–Keith

Answer

It's true. Between my wife and myself (joint accounts) we have over 80 credit cards!

WARNING, I am NOT advising anyone to go and get 80 credit cards! The more credit lines you have available, the greater the probability you'll increase your debt, obviously.

So why do I have so many cards?

There are many reasons:

1) When I borrow money I want to have many loan options. About half of my accounts are offering me low-rate transfer deals all the time! I have purchased used cars with my credit cards at 0%! And because I have so many cards I can continue to transfer the balances and keep the rates less than 4% all the time. I've been doing that for more than 10 years!

2) I'm into this topic, saving money on credit cards. How can I write about credit cards if I don't have credit cards? How can I verify good credit card offers if I don't ever receive or use any?

3) I actually enjoy trying to uncover the true costs of credit. I need lots-o-data!

4) Who would you want writing about credit...someone who hasn't had or used a credit card for 25 years or somebody who deals with credit cards all the time?

I don't carry a balance on all of those credit cards. If I did, then this article would be about bankruptcy not being "debt smart."

If you think 80 credit cards are a lot then how many do you think the worlds record is?

According to the Guinness Book of World Records Walter Cavanagh of Santa Clara, CA is "Mr. Plastic Fantastic" and blows me away with a total of 1,397 unique accounts! I couldn't even image juggling that many credit cards.

Next, your strategy for using a card that gives you perks, at 0% for purchases, is good. You used the perk card then transferred the balance to a low rate card. When you were done you closed all the accounts. That's great!

I personally don't close the accounts as long as the banks aren't charging me an annual fee. I keep them open because they ALWAYS give me a great offer within a couple months after my balance goes to zero. I don't want to keep applying for new accounts and closing accounts.

It is true that you're going to have a difficult time getting a mortgage if you have many open credit lines—even if the balances are zero. That's because the bank doesn't want you to have the potential to get into credit card trouble since it could affect their mortgage profits.

How many cards are too many?

When you apply for a mortgage the bank may ask you to close some credit card accounts before they grant you a mortgage. Each bank has it's own lending policies. When I purchased my home I had 24 credit card accounts and I got the mortgage with no problem and no questions asked.

As far as having a greater chance of becoming a victim of fraud, I doubt the number of cards is going to make you a greater target.

Actually, when you think about it, someone would have a difficult time getting new credit in my name. If they tried they'd probably get rejected because I have so many accounts right now. If I only had 2 accounts open then it would be much easier for someone to defraud me with identity theft. Ironic isn't it?

And since I don't carry all those credit cards with me, I only carry 2 in my wallet, I don't have to worry about losing the actual cards. Also, I keep a list of all the items in my wallet just in case I do ever lose it. Plus I have every account and every phone number in a database so I can contact each bank if there ever was a problem.

You said that you don't see the point to having that many credit cards. The point is a personal point, Scott's choice, for Scott's reasons. It works for me and may not work for everyone. I attribute getting out of debt to having all those credit cards. I learned how to beat the system by being immersed in it and developing good *Credit Card and Debt Management.*

Every Penny Counts

It sure does-especially when you're paying back debt.

How many times have you walked out into the parking lot of a supermarket and spotted a penny on the ground? Plenty of times no doubt. You might bend over to pick one up if you see Lincoln staring at you, but for the most part you just keep walking by.

I mean after all, with the cost of inflation over the years, what is a penny worth? It really isn't worth that much as far as buying something tangible like a television, is it? What's a penny going to add toward that purchase (besides one cent)?

I remember when, for a penny, you could get a gumball. My father can remember going to the movies for pennies. Now people leave their pennies at the counter of the convenience store to help the next person balance their transaction. And why? So they don't have to get any pennies in their change! My point is that the penny doesn't seem to have much value, but it certainly has value when you're dealing with your loans.

When it comes to paying back your debt, a penny can mean a lot. Applying one extra cent to each payment can make a significant difference in how much you repay over time. Let's walk through an example that clearly demonstrates exactly how valuable the penny can be.

The example loan is $10,000 at 18% and you're making monthly payments of $150.

Question:
How long does it take to repay this loan?

Answer:
You can never repay that loan by making payments of $150 per month.

No matter how many payments you make, you will always owe $10,000-forever! Why? The amount of monthly interest is exactly equal to how much you're paying. That monthly interest fee is $150 ($10,000 x 0.18 ₁ 12). You'll never owe any more than $10,000, but you'll never be able to pay off the loan.

Next question:
What happens if you add just one penny to that payment? Just one cent? That's right, now the payment becomes a big $150.01. Now how long will it take to pay back that loan?

Answer:
It takes 53 years, 10 months! Okay, that's a lifetime for some people, or at least half a lifetime. Now, because of that one penny, instead of paying $150 until death (forever), the loan is eventually paid off.

Okay, so you don't want to be in debt for almost 54 years. What can you do?

You guessed it. Add another penny.

So here's the next question:
How much do you save by making payments of $150.02?

Answer:

It now takes exactly 50 years to pay back the loan! That extra penny knocked almost 4 years off the payback time of the loan. How much money did that extra penny save? Let's see, the out-of-pocket cost of the first loan is $150.01 for 53 years, 10 months. That comes to a total repayment of $96,884.72 (the last payment is less than $150.01).

With the extra penny, payments of $150.02 for 50 years, it costs a total of $89,907.69. That's a savings of $6,977.03! Quite a bit saved just for adding a single penny.

Think about this.. by increasing the payment from $150.01 to $150.02 you are adding one cent for 50 years. Well, 50 years is 600 months (600 extra pennies) or an out-of-pocket increase of just $6 over the course of that time in order to save $6,977.03 in the end. Pretty neat-I think.

Okay, I hear the arguments mounting. "But Scott, that's a crazy example, who's really going to get a loan for 54 years?"

My answer is that many people are doing it right now! How? By making the minimum payment each month. If you charge $8,000 on a credit card at 19.8% APR (annual percentage rate) and continuously make the minimum payment it takes 54 years to pay it back!

Remember, the bottom line is the more you can pay back, early on, the more you can save in the end. So the next time you see a penny laying in the road somewhere, you may want to think twice before passing it by.

Refinancing Secrets Uncovered

You may be thinking of refinancing since interest rates are lower than ever. But with all the costs, application fees, points, etc. how can you be sure you're getting the best deal? Can you be sure that it's better than your current loan?

There are many "rules of thumb" that may or may not apply to your situation, like, "if the new mortgage is at least 2% less than the existing mortgage, it's good to refinance," but that may not always be true. Other variables become significantly important depending on your specific situation. For example, you may want to roll some other debts into a new mortgage or you may be going from a 30-year loan to a 15-year loan.

My philosophy is that the best loan is the cheapest loan. No matter where you "buy" your money it's still the same—little green pieces of paper with pictures. The only thing that separates one loan from another is its cost, that is, the fees compared to other loan options.

Since your situation is probably more complicated than any one online calculator can handle, you have probably asked a few trusted friends their opinions about whether "to refinance or not," or which loan to pick. However, there is much more to it than a simple answer. Here's a short example of a loan I analyzed for my friend, José.

Refinance Question:

I have a loan for $15,500 at 12.25% for 20 years. I have the opportunity to refinance at 9.5%. The problem is that they want to charge me $1,700 as a processing fee. This will bring the loan amount to $17,200 at 9.5% for 20 years (although I'm only keeping 15,500). Is it worth it?

Summary of Analysis:

There are a few ways to look at your refinance. First, we can say that you're going to borrow $17,200 at 9.5% for 20 years and make payments of $160.33. Of course, you really don't get $17,200, you get $15,500 to pay off the other loan.

So it's like getting a loan of $15,500 and paying $160.33 for 20 years. The corresponding APR for that principal, payment, and time is 11.03%. In the long run you're really refinancing from 12.25% to 11.03%. That seems okay but now let's look at it another way.

With your current loan it takes payments of $173.38 for 20 years to pay off the loan. We can compare that payment amount to the new loan and say that you're going to make the same payment, $173.38, to the $17,200 at 9.5%. In this comparison we're not changing anything about your current position. You're paying the same amounts as you are now but to the new loan.

In this case it takes 64 payments before the 9.5% loan "looks like" the 12.25% loan because of the $1,700 up-front fee. In other words, after 64 payments the unpaid balance of the new loan is the same as it would be after 64th payment under the old loan. Every payment after 64 brings down the true rate of the loan, which after 20 years, will get as low as 11.25%.

Based on how you repay the loan the true rate is between 11.03% and 11.25% at best and you save approximately $3,132 in out-of-pocket costs over 20 years (the difference between the payments). However, you'll really save about $6,120 in true dollars because that WOULD have been your unpaid balance if you continued making the same payments as today, but toward the new loan, since it is now paid off by the 196th payment.

The bottom line, as long as you ARE NOT going to pay off the loan with another refinance, or with cash, before the 64th payment, then it's going to be "better" (cheaper) than your current loan, after the 64th payment.

Pay Off Debt with Your Clutter

You know all the stuff that's filling up your garage, attic, or shed? It's the same stuff that you want to sell at a garage sale if you only had the time. Well, those unwanted items may be able to help you start reducing your debt today!

How?

By selling it all at online auctions like eBay.com. Although I have been recommending doing this for years, I've only recently started selling my unwanted household clutter online. It's really not clutter it's stuff I don't want anymore that other people might need.

Since I'm just getting started selling at online auctions I'm also going to start letting everyone know about how I'm doing it and how well it's going.

So far, it's going VERY well! Everything I've put online has sold! I've sold an autographed Norman Mailer book that my father picked up at the library discard rack and a digital voice recorder. Total sales, $56.00 for two hours of work—that's $23 per hour for creating more space in my garage! Pretty good deal!

To make transactions simple, you can receive payment from your auctions through PayPal. They allow your buyers to use their credit cards to pay. Setting up an account with PayPal is FREE, however, there are modest transaction charges.

I've already auctioned off a Sony Handycam Video 8mm CCD-F33, videocamera.

How can you get started making extra money today?

Look through your house for items you believe may be worth selling. Items that you can probably sell for $10 or more.

Next, research the value of your item. Go to eBay.com and do a search for your item. Check the current items for sale and the completed items. Look at the prices that your item has sold for in the past so you can get an idea of its true sale value. Also, read what other people wrote about that item so you have a starting point for writing your advertising copy (fancy way of saying "sales pitch").

Market Research

Remember that camera I put up for auction? Well, it sold for $71! That's $71 off my debt! So far, everything I've put up for auction has sold.

Look through your house for stuff that you really don't use anymore. That stuff may be very useful to other people, so you should consider selling it online at auction web sites like eBay.com and use the proceeds to reduce your debts.

Once you find items that are good candidates to be sold online, it is important to be able to get an idea of how much they are worth. You can look at StrongNumbers.com for prices of many items, or simply go to eBay.com and do a search for the items.

By reviewing the search results, you'll find the best description for your item. Do another search with the more specific description and see if any are for sale right now.

Next, click on "completed items" which will show you what your item has sold for in the past. Then sort by highest price first. This final research list tells you the highest prices you can expect to get when you auction your item. It also tells you what people used in their description that made the item sell at the greatest price. This is the information you'll want to include in your item description.

Finally, you need to register with eBay.com to get an account. The registration process is easy. Just go to their main page and click on "register now," and fill out the online forms.

Okay, so now you have the item, you have an idea of what to write in the description, you have an account, the next thing you need is a picture of the item.

As the cliché goes, "a picture is worth a thousand words," and this is absolutely true! People want to see what they're going to buy. When you were researching the item description, you should also have noticed the photos used. You'll want to take similar pictures to use in your description.

The best way to get great photos is with a digital camera. I use the Sony Digital Mavica FD73 ($350). Another option is to take a film photo and scan the print.

Also, many companies that process film give you the option of having your pictures posted online. This option allows you to take pictures of your items, then download the pictures. You can then use the pictures that are already posted online to link in the HTML description of your item (I'll talk about that in the next column).

Research your items, pick the most likely to sell, take a photo of each item, and make each picture digital.

Posting Your Items

You should be ready to:

1) Identify items you're ready to sell online.
2) Research the value of each item.
3) Develop the "sales copy," i.e. the words you use in the item description.
4) Take photos of each item and digitized them.

Now all you need to do is post the items.

Quick mention, all the stuff I had for sale last week sold! So far 100% of my items have sold and taken over $150 off my debt! My latest sale is a Star Trek book that I found at the flea market for $5.

Two final notes before we get to posting your items.

First, you need to determine how much shipping may be for your items. You must decide how much to charge, if you're going to include it in the final price at no additional cost or if you'll let the auction winner know the shipping costs at the end of the auction.

Second, you need to be able to accept payment. Many people will want to pay with a credit card. The good news is that you don't have to set up a merchant account. You can simply sign up with PayPal.com.

Back to posting...

There are many online auctions where you can sell your items. The most popular place is eBay.com so we'll talk about posting there.

To post your items go to eBay.com and click on "sell" on the top menu bar then select a category.

TIP: You can enter a category number at the bottom, which is a great short cut, however, you need to know the number. To quickly get the category number for your item, go to an auction for a similar item. Directly below the Item # is a link to the category. When you click on this link look at the URL. The category number is shown in the URL, for example, ".../list/category11724/..." this is a great short cut for finding the category.

Next you need to enter a title for your auction. Again, look at the research you did with similar items. Use the same description that others have used.

Use the same strategy for the description, look at what others have written for similar items. Be careful to not copy the exact wording in the description because this may technically be a violation of copyrights—just paraphrase.

You're allowed to post one photo for free with your auction. Take advantage of this! Also, for only an additional 25 cents you can have your photo shown in the line-item listing—I do this every time.

Another important decision is setting the minimum bid price. "Your auction will start at this price: generally, it is the lowest price at which you are willing to sell. Setting the minimum bid too high may discourage bidding!"

If nobody bids to your minimum price then you don't have to sell the item.

Finish completing the posting information. For a basic posting the default settings are probably going to be correct. There are many sections of this form so READ everything very carefully.

After you have correctly completed the form you'll be quoted the price for listing your auction. Be sure that the price makes sense. For listing a $10 item the cost is approximately $1.25. Be sure to print this page for your records.

Good Luck!

Great Deals You Can Find in the Classified Ads

Many people run directly to the store to buy brand new items at full price when there are many other options. In fact, one of the best options we've found is shopping for items through classified ads. That's why we've just started the DebtSmart® Online Classified section so you can shop for items and services plus post stuff to sell.

You have probably used classified ads in the past for numerous reasons however, we want to tell you about one of our best experiences and remind everyone that you can save BIG money by shopping for "pre-owned" merchandise rather than running out to buy new all the time.

One of the best deals we found using classified ads is sitting beautifully in our dining room right now!

As newlyweds, we wanted brand new furniture for our apartment. For some reason we thought if it were new it would be of better quality. But nearly a decade later not only did our taste in style change, but the furniture was looking quite shabby.

We decided to replace the dining room set, and this time we knew better than to go to the store first. We searched through the classified ad sections of all our local newspapers for used dining room tables.

There were certain requirements for the new table such as: (1) solid wood, (2) no upholstered chairs, too easily stained by children, (3) seat at least six people, (4) be in good condition, (5) high quality, and (6) must be a great deal, financially.

We searched and searched. We visited many people and looked at their tables, but they weren't exactly what we had in mind. Discouraged, we went looking in the furniture stores. The closest we found to match our criteria was a Broyhill that seated six and was about $1,200 with the chairs. Yikes! We did want a high quality table, but that just seemed like too high a price. We looked in numerous furniture stores and noticed that the prices and quality were not getting better.

After about two weeks of looking in the stores, we decided to give the classifieds another try before giving up and buying a new table. Well, as you have guessed, we found someone selling a great table at a great price. They were moving to Florida and didn't want to haul everything with them during the move.

The table was everything we had hoped to find. It's an Ethan Allen, solid oak, two leaves, with eight chairs! It was in such great condition that many people thought it was new. The price for this set—$700! What a deal! After doing some research we found that similar chairs, brand new, from the same manufacturer, retail around $349 each. So for eight new chairs only, the cost would be about $2,800!

Searching the classified ads turned out to be well worth the time and effort in this case. By the way, we financed the $700 table by using a no fee, cash advance, from one of our credit cards at a rate of 2.99%.

In the past we've also turned to the classifieds to buy and sell cars, find jobs, buy other furniture, and learn about other sales. At a recent church sale that we learned about through the classifieds, we purchased a sleeper sofa (seats three), love seat, twin-size cot, entertainment center, five-drawer dresser, and storage end table, for only $195 which included delivery to a second-floor apartment!

So the next time that you're getting ready to make a major purchase like a television, table, or car, be sure to look in your local newspaper's classified section. Also, if you're selling an item or have a service that can help people, you'll want to consider placing a classified ad in your local paper.

CHAPTER 7

MORTGAGES

"If you know the future, then today's decision is very clear."—Scott Bilker, 2001

Biweekly Mortgages May Be A Rip-Off.

Biweekly mortgages have been touted by many companies as being an excellent way to save money and pay off your mortgage earlier. Some companies even claim that "it won't cost you any more than you're paying now." What a crock! What do you think a true biweekly mortgage saves you? I'm talking about the savings from paying more frequently. Well, it doesn't save that much at all. Hold on to your calculators, we're going to use our brains and look at this problem very carefully. Here is something these biweekly mortgage salespeople don't want you to do.

A $100,000 mortgage at 8% for 30 years has a monthly payment of $733.76. That's 360 payments of $733.76 or a total of $264,155 at the end of 30 years. A true biweekly mortgage with 780 payments (26 payments per year) has a payment of $338.52, which totals $264,041 after 30 years of payments. Check out how much you saved by paying biweekly, that's right, only 114 bucks ($264,155-$264,041)!

So, if paying more frequently isn't what creates the savings, how can these companies claim to save you big money? They use the "biweekly" word to imply that increased frequency of payment can save money when the real way they show the savings is by making you increase your payments.

They do a little math trick to force you to pay more, and that trick is to divide your mortgage in half and make that result the biweekly payment. The problem here is that 26 half-payments equal 13 whole-payments or an extra month's payment each year. Obviously, if you pay more money, you reduce your mortgage faster.

Let's go back to my original example. Notice that half the monthly payment of $733.76 is $366.88. If you pay $366.88 every two weeks, it only takes around 23 years to repay the $100,000 and costs a total of $217,853. So it seems like you save money by paying more frequently, but in reality it's the extra money that reduces the mortgage faster.

This is a forced-discipline mortgage repayment plan. Not only requiring you to increase your payment, but how frequently you make those payments. Under the biweekly mortgage plan you make 26 payments per year instead of 12. Now you're writing 14 more checks each year. Isn't that fun, yeah, just what you always wanted, 14 more bills to pay each year! And to gain what? Nothing you can't do yourself.

But the stupidity of this scheme doesn't end here. Most biweekly mortgage companies actually want to charge you for this entire setup! That's right, most companies charge an up-front fee and a monthly service fee.

The monthly service fee is so they can debit your checking account every two weeks and you don't have to write the checks. That sounds to me to be an advantage for them! They get your money guaranteed since they can take it from your account at will. I think you should charge them a fee for that privilege!

Recently, a company attempted to sell my uncle on refinancing his current mortgage into one of these biweekly farces. Get this, their interest rate was higher than his current mortgage! But, the saleswomen argued, "interest rates don't matter... look at how much you save."

"Interest rates don't matter!" How can she get away with that direct lie?

Let's look at the numbers. Refer again to my first example of $100,000 for 30 years at 8% with a monthly payment of $733.76 that costs a total of $264,155 to repay. She said something like, "even though the biweekly payment is $366.88 (half the monthly payment) you can afford to add a little more... how about another $50? That raises your biweekly payment to $416.88."

Her company's rate is 9% and with payments of $416.88 ($366.88+$50) the total cost to repay the $100,000 is $214,026. The savings look like $50,128 (the difference between $264,155 and $214,026). Then there's the $500 up-front fee and the $3 per-payment fee that they don't include in the total cost of the loan.

So how much would this truly cost my uncle if he signed up for this rip-off plan? When you include all the fees of the biweekly plan it comes to $216,068. He always has the option to pay $903.24 monthly toward his current mortgage. That $903.24 monthly payment is the equivalent of paying $416.88 biweekly. At $903.24 he can pay his current mortgage off for a total cost of $182,093. And that's with no special plan, fees, extra payments or, in other words, no smoke and mirrors.

Look at that figure ($182,093). They tried to sucker him into complex financial scheme that would cost $216,068! That rip-off plan would have him pay nearly an extra $34,000 compared to doing it on his own!

There are also considerations, such as other debts. If you have credit-card debts with interest rates greater than your mortgage rate; it makes sense to pay back the credit cards first. Similarly, if you have investments earning more than the interest rate of your mortgage, it's best to continue investing. Also, because of inflation, your future payments toward your mortgage are less when compared to current dollars. For example, my parents' mortgage payment was $198 when they purchased their home in 1969. This amount was a lot for that time but doesn't seem like much now. The good news is that your $800 mortgage payment will seem like peanuts in 30 years.

Let's look at the pros and cons of the biweekly mortgage through third-party companies. Cons: (1) probably costs far more than doing it yourself, (2) more CON-fusion, (3) forces you to pay earlier, (4) less flexibility in mortgage payments. Pros: (1) Gee, I can't think of any... I guess if you want to be forced to pay off your mortgage early, and enjoy giving someone a fee to force you to, then it's good.

My opinion is that if you want to pay your mortgage off early and save money on interest, then add some extra money to your monthly payment. This way, if for some reason you have trouble making the new payment, you always have the option to make the old lower payment, plus you retain more control over your money.

Or if you really want to be forced to pay your mortgage off early then ask you current bank if they can set up a direct payment plan that includes your extra principal payment. As long as they can do this for free then give it a try.

Q&A: Second Mortgage?

Question

Dear Scott,
        We want to purchase a new truck in a few weeks and are undecided on how we wish to finance it. We have plenty of equity in our home. Would it be economical to take out a second mortgage (approx. $28,000) for this purchase? Also, wouldn't the interest be tax deductible? A few years ago we obtained a second mortgage to pay off some high interest credit cards and was unable to deduct the interest. Of course we would shop around for the best rate and will compare closing costs. My questions are:
        1. What are your thoughts on a second mortgage for a truck purchase.
        2. What range is considered "good" for interest rates?
        3. What can we expect to pay in closing costs for a second mortgage in the amount of $28,000?
Thanks!
—Debbie

Answer

Debbie,
Thanks for writing!
        The only thing that makes one loan better than another is the cost. A second mortgage is a loan with a fancy name and some tax advantages. To find the comparable rate for a non-tax advantage loan, simply subtract your tax bracket from 1 and multiply by the second mortgage rate.
        For example, if you're in the 15% tax bracket and you take a 9% APR second mortgage, it's the same as a 7.65% APR credit card, personal, or car loan, (1-0.15)*9=7.65, when reduced by the tax benefit.
        So if you can finance the car through the dealer, without them ripping you off somehow, for 2% or whatever their new-car financing deal is, you will be better off.

What are your thoughts on a second mortgage for a truck purchase?
        As long as it costs less, then I may do it. The only thing is that you're putting your house up as collateral for the car.

What range is considered "good" for interest rates?
        A good rate is the best rate you can get. The national average for mortgages are between 7% and 9%.

What can we expect to pay in closing costs for a second mortgage in the amount of $28,000?
        I wouldn't accept any closing costs for that loan. There are so many banks that would be willing to give you a second mortgage with no closing costs. Just keep looking. Also, you may do better financing the car through the dealer, or your current bank, with a new car loan.
        The bottom line is to look into all your options. Calculate the cost of each loan and pick the best deal.
        Good luck and keep in touch!
—Scott

Q&A: Adjustable Mortgage

Question

Dear Scott,
Our credit isn't too good. My husband had open heart surgery about a year ago and lost three months of work. We have some 30-60 days late. How do we get our credit back into order. Also our home is 100% financed. We have a adjustable rate on our mortgage. How do they decide if the rate goes up or down. How is it calculated and when? Every quarter? Thanks for your time.
—Nellie

Answer

Nellie,

Glad to hear that your husband is doing well after heart surgery.

The best way to start getting your credit back in order is to contact the banks and let them now what's going on. Ask them to make payment arrangements that you can handle, also ask them if they can remove those late payment comments from your credit report.

The basic ARM (adjustable rate mortgage) adjusts the interest once a year, three years, or five years. However, some may have special conditions so you'll need to look at your mortgage agreement to know the exact terms. Interest rates can be based on a variety of interest indexes, so again, you'll need to look at your specific mortgage but that information should be easily found in the original paperwork.

As far as saving money on the mortgage goes, it always seems that banks are much quicker to raise rates than to lower them. Right now is a great time to start looking into refinancing that mortgage to a lower fixed rate. That's because many financial experts believe that rates will decline further this month.

Good luck and please let me know what happens.

—Scott

Q&A: Buying a House After Bankruptcy

Question 1

Scott,
How hard is it to buy a house after filing for chapter seven bankruptcy? How long will it take to get a house? What are some of the things I need to do before even going to try to buy a house?
—Rachel

Answer 1

Rachel,

First let me say that bankruptcy is certainly not the end of your credit life. I know many people that have filed bankruptcy and went on to rebuild their credit very quickly—and buy a house!

Bankruptcy will show up on your credit report for 10 years. That means that every mortgage lender will certainly see that fact when evaluating your mortgage application.

Although it may be difficult to find a bank to give you a mortgage it's certainly not impossible. Banks want to make money and you may find one that's willing to take the risk. You can increase your chances by coming into the deal with as much cash as possible. The more money you can use as a down payment, the less risk for the bank. There is a level where they'll lend you the money because the loan is secured by the house and the house is worth more than the mortgage.

In summary, cash will solve this problem, for sure. However long it takes to gather that cash is how long it will take to get the house. I would shoot for at least 20% down.

I'm guessing that you don't have that kind of money or you wouldn't have filed for Chapter 7 in the first place but now that you have a clean slate it's time to start building your wealth, saving, and getting ready for that house.

Start thinking about how you can make money in your spare time, selling on line at eBay, doing freelance work, or starting your own business.

Good luck and please let me know what happens.

—Scott

Q&A: Debt Reduction vs. Mortgage Down Payment

Question

Dear Scott,

My husband and I are in debt for about 28k and have recently sold our home. We are looking to buy a more expensive house in a better neighborhood and school district for our two kids to start school in. I am currently working a lot of overtime, but am not sure if I should try to payoff some of the debt or save for a down payment. Could you please help me??

—Anna

Answer

Anna,

Great question! Actually, I was in this exact, and I mean exact debt too, situation when I purchased my house.

The answer is to save for the down payment.

If I could do it any way I want, I would prefer to pay back the debt then cash advance the down payment for the house but you can't do that. You must have a down payment from you own money to buy a house. You can have money gifted to you by family members and even borrow from your 401(k) to get the down payment. One thing you cannot do is borrow money for the down payment from credit cards.

Save, save, save.

Good luck with your new house!

—Scott

Question 2

Scott,
Thanks for the info! I just want to clarify something...

We are going to borrow from my husband's 401k and we do have some savings, but should I try to save to get to a 20% down payment and have no remaining money, or should I just pay off stuff to lower my monthly bills and put down less than 20%?

Thanks!

—Anna

Answer 2

Anna,

I would save for the 20% down payment. It sounds like your close and there is the benefit of not having to pay for mortgage insurance when you put 20% down.

Regards,

—Scott

Q&A: Saving for a Down Payment

Question

Scott,

How do you save money to buy a home when you are swamped with credit card bills that just seem to suck every last bit of savings?

—Darryl

Answer

Darryl,

I know exactly how you feel since I was in that very same position at one time.

First of all you need to be sure that your credit card interest rates are as low as possible. By "low" I mean below 11.9%. There are many excellent credit-card offers available from numerous banks, which make the rates very competitive. Look through your junk mail and read the fine print in some of those offers. Start using the 0% offers and track the dates when they expire so you can be sure to transfer your balance before the rate is increased.

Once you've minimized your interest cost, you need to make saving for that house a priority. The way I saved while paying my credit card bills was to make minimum payments. That's right, it's one of those exceptions to the pay-the-most-to-your-credit-cards- first-rule.

In this case, to save for the down payment of your house, you make the minimum payments to your credit cards and bank the difference. The reason is that you need to save your own money to use as a down payment; you cannot cash advance money from your credit cards to buy a house. Well I guess, technically you could, but most likely you won't be given a mortgage if the bank learns that you're buying a house with your credit cards.

The strategy here is that you're going create extra money by paying less each month to your credit cards. Many times banks will give you an opportunity to skip a payment. That's the perfect time to save that extra payment in a bank account toward your down payment.

Many people would criticize me for suggesting that you pay less to your credit cards because you're going to pay a little extra interest. However, this interest cost is the fee you pay to be able to get the cash for the house. It was worth it for me and everything turned out just fine.

Good luck and please let me know how things go!

—Scott

INDEX

Your Personal DebtSmart® Notes